From the pages of
Model Railroader
MAGAZINE

Basic
Model Railroading
Getting Started in the Hobby

KALMBACH
BOOKS

Printed in the United States of America

98 99 00 01 02 03 04 05 06 07   10 9 8 7 6 5 4 3 2 1

For more information, visit our website at
http://www.kalmbach.com

Publisher's Cataloging-in-Publication
(Provided by Quality Books, Inc.)

Basic model railroading : getting started in the hobby /
    [edited by Kent J. Johnson]. — 1st ed.
        p.   cm.
        ISBN: 0-89024-334-4

    1. Railroads—Models. I. Johnson, Kent J., 1968– II.
Model railroader.

    TF197.B37 1998   625.1´9
                                      QBI98-309

Cover design: Kristi Ludwig

The material in this book has previously appeared as articles in *Model Railroader* Magazine. They are reprinted in their entirety and include an occasional reference to an item elsewhere in the same issue or in a previous issue.

CONTENTS

Questions and answers for beginners

Introducing a new series for modelers just entering the hobby

BY JEFF WILSON

Every holiday season thousands of potential model railroaders receive trains as gifts, and many more go out and purchase model trains for themselves. For this reason, our December issue has traditionally included several articles and columns aimed at newcomers.

We thought this issue would be a great time to kick off a new series, called Basic Model Railroading. Each month we'll explore a different topic, such as scenery, wiring, and trackwork, with articles focused toward modelers just getting into the hobby.

New modelers usually have lots of questions, so we'll devote the first installment to answering some of the most-asked ones:

Is a train set the best way to get started?

Train sets are handy because their ready-to-run locomotive and cars, together with a loop of track and a power pack, provide all that you need to be up and running in minutes.

The big disadvantage of most commercial train sets is low quality. To keep prices down, many sets have sub-par locomotives. Many have unrealistic paint jobs, oversize details, poor-running motors, and are powered by (and pick up electricity from) only half their wheels. Also, wheelsets on cars and locomotives can be out of gauge, making them track poorly.

One notable exception is the new Walthers Trainline HO set, which we're happy to recommend. Micro-Trains Line offers quality N scale sets that feature the firm's freight cars, Atlas or Kato locomotives, and Atlas track.

The best place to buy a train set is a hobby shop. You stand a better chance of getting good equipment, and most shops will be able to answer questions and service what they sell. General merchandise stores don't service train sets, and once the holiday season is over the trains will be gone. Also, at a hobby shop you'll be able to explore other accessories, individual pieces of rolling stock, locomotives, scenery materials, books, and other items.

Is there an alternative to starting with a packaged train set?

You can put your own set together without paying much more than for many commercial sets. Here's a sample HO set: Start with an Athearn four-axle locomotive, four or five easy-to-assemble freight car kits from Accurail or

Athearn, and a caboose with the same road name as the locomotive. Add an oval of Atlas code 100 nickel-silver track and a small power pack from Bachmann Spectrum or Model Rectifier Corp., and you'll be set.

You won't be able to run trains immediately, as you'll have to assemble the cars. However, you'll have good-running equipment, the pride and experience of having built something yourself, and you'll be able to keep and use the equipment on future layouts.

TRACK CLEANING

When I first set everything up my locomotive ran great, but after letting it sit for a few days it ran rather jerkily. Is this caused by dirty track? What can I do about it?

To start with, use nickel-silver track instead of brass. Both metals oxidize, but the oxidation that forms on brass is non-conductive while the oxidation on nickel-silver is a conductor.

Usually the best way to clean track, especially on a small layout, is with an abrasive track-cleaning block (such as a Bright Boy) and some elbow grease. Don't use sandpaper – it will leave scratches that will collect grime and reduce conductivity.

What's the best way to start a layout?

Begin simply by setting up your track on a table or sheet of plywood – 4 x 8-foot sheets are handy. Buy some extra track sections and a couple of turnouts (track switches), and experiment with different track arrangements.

When you feel you're ready to build a layout, start small – no larger than 4 x 8. Many modelers make the mistake of trying to do too much too soon. A small layout enables you to quickly experience several facets of the hobby – track-laying, building structures, scenery – without being overwhelmed. It also lets you see a layout through to completion fairly soon.

You should resist the temptation to cram as much track as possible into a layout. The result is usually poor operation with no room for scenery, structures, and other details. It's a good idea to start with a published plan from a magazine or book. Once you've worked on a small layout or two, you'll be much better prepared to tackle a larger empire.

I want to control two trains at once on the same oval of track. Can I buy a second power pack and attach it to the track?

Bad advice: Micro-Trains are high quality not. Recommended Brand Train Sets

Bad advice RTR freight or passenger cars not mentioned.

2 Trains
See Cab Control
see Kalmach's
RR wiring

Hobby shops are great places to check out new and exciting products. This is the G scale corner of the Hobby Horse in Brookfield, Wis.

Running two trains isn't quite that easy, but it's not difficult, either. To run more than one train requires the use of electrical switches to control various sections of track. We'll explain basic cab control in a future installment, but in the meantime I can recommend the Kalmbach book *Your Guide to Easy Model Railroad Wiring.*

What tools will I need to build structure and car kits and work on models?

Hobby knives are probably the most-used tools. I keep two handy: X-acto handles with no. 11 (pointed) and no. 17 (chisel-end) blades.

You'll need a scale rule with markings for N, HO, S, and O scales on it. You'll find it handy for converting drawings in other scales to your scale. A National Model Railroad Association standards gauge is a must for checking that track and wheelsets are gauged properly.

Other important tools include tweezers, needle files, a set of small screwdrivers, needlenose pliers, side-cutting pliers, small paint brushes, soldering iron, and a razor saw.

How can I learn more about the various facets of the hobby?

Z + Gare is ignored

Books are great references for specialized areas such as scenery and wiring because they can go into far more detail than any single magazine article. Kalmbach Publishing Co. publishes a variety of how-to books on scenery, wiring, track planning, structures, and other topics. Magazine articles are a great source of ideas for individual modeling projects.

I know that HO is the most popular scale, but what's the best scale for a first layout?

That's a tough question that modelers must answer for themselves. This month's Trackside Photos column includes views of six modeling scales. Looking at these will give you an idea of what can be done in each one.

To help you sort out this question, next month's Basic Model Railroading will look at the various scales, highlighting the advantages of each. ♦

Ducks the posted question

Understanding scale and gauge

Choosing a size is the first step to model railroading fun

BY PETE WICKLUND

(handwritten margin notes) Aristo Craft has 1:29 · Poor! In practice Xn3 means Vertical X lower on the next track · Regular gauge · n3 means narrow gauge · There is On3 HO n3 Sn3 · TT · OO · Checking where are they covered?

Scale model railroad cars and locomotives run the gamut in size, from those that will rest on your forefinger to some you can actually mount and ride. Deciding on a scale will depend on your preference, of course, but also on your budget, available space, and modeling skills.

This doesn't mean you can't change your mind down the road. Many modelers start in one scale and turn to another

gauge track. For example, HOn3 means that the HO track being discussed is only a scale 3 feet wide, rather than the standard 4'-8½". Locomotives and cars are smaller and use wheelsets gauged to fit this track, but trackside accessories and structures are the same 1:87 proportion of HO scale.

O and S scales

Toy electric trains have been around since the 19th century, but popularity, reliability, and mass production didn't take hold until early this century. Toy train manufacturers around 1900 began making track in various widths that for marketing purposes were numbered, such as No. 1, No. 2, and No. 3. In 1910 the Ives Co. came out with a track narrower than the No. 1 size and the company called the new product 0 (zero) gauge. The size caught on in popularity, much in part due to the tinplate products offered by companies like Lionel and Marx, and over time it came to be called O ("oh") gauge.

S scale similarly has its roots in toy production. American Flyer trains, from which today's S scale trains evolved, were a common fixture of the 1940s and 1950s. The marketing thought behind American Flyer was that the 1:64 scale products would be truer to real trains than O gauge toys, yet not be too small to discourage toy shoppers. Today O and S scales remain in both toy and scale incarnations.

About 6 percent of today's scale modelers list O as their primary scale, while 1 percent are in S. These scales appeal to modelers who enjoy the level of detail larger equipment can showcase. A downside to both scales is that the scope of products is somewhat limited, moreso in S scale than in O. As a result, many modelers in these scales turn to specialty clubs and publications to find the equipment and accessories they need, and frequently build needed items from scratch.

POPULAR MODEL RAILROADING SCALES

Name	Proportion	Scale to foot	Track gauge	Minimum radius*	Length of a scale mile
Z	1:220	1.4 mm	6.5 mm	5¾"	24'-0"
N	1:160	1.9 mm	9.0 mm	7½"	33'-0"
HO	1:87	3.5 mm	16.5 mm	15"	60'-7½"
S	1:64	³⁄₁₆"	⅞"	22½"	82'-6"
O	1:48	¼"	1¼"	23"	110'-0"
Gn3	1:22.5	12.5 mm	1¾" (No. 1)	23⅝"	234'-8"

*based on smallest radius sectional track available

later in their modeling careers. And don't let space limitations skew your judgment. MODEL RAILROADER has recently run several articles on small layouts built in some of the more popular larger scales.

Defining scale and gauge

As you enter the hobby you'll hear these two words mentioned a lot; indeed people sometimes incorrectly interchange these terms.

Scale, plain and simple, refers to the proportion of the model in comparison with the real thing. So when we say HO ("aitch oh") scale is 1:87, we're saying an HO model is 87 times smaller than what you'd find on a real (or prototype) railroad.

In the accompanying chart we've listed the most common modeling scales and their proportion to prototype railroading. Some models are built in scales even larger than G, but we don't often cover these in MODEL RAILROADER.

Gauge refers to the width of the track, measured between the railheads. Just as there has been standardization in model railroading, real railroads more than a hundred years ago set standards so their cars could be interchanged to move passengers and goods throughout the country. The standard track gauge of prototype railroads in North America is 4'-8½".

In model railroading if the scale is listed solely by its letter designation (N, HO, or O) you can assume the model track is standard gauge. So the width of standard HO track is ⅟87th the width of real track and N scale is ⅟160th.

Narrow gauge track has the rails closer together than standard gauge. In the real world you can find narrow gauge track in places where geography places restraints on constructing and operating railroads, like on mountains, in quarries, and in forests.

In modeling, when you see the scale letter followed by a small letter "n" and some numerals, this indicates narrow

HO scale

Today's most popular scale is HO, so named because it's roughly half the size of O scale. This scale was developed in the 1930s when Depression-era budgets had modelers searching for trains that could run on a layout in tight quarters.

After World War II the popularity of HO exploded and surpassed O scale. Today about 74 percent of modelers are in HO and the wide availability of products is a reflection of

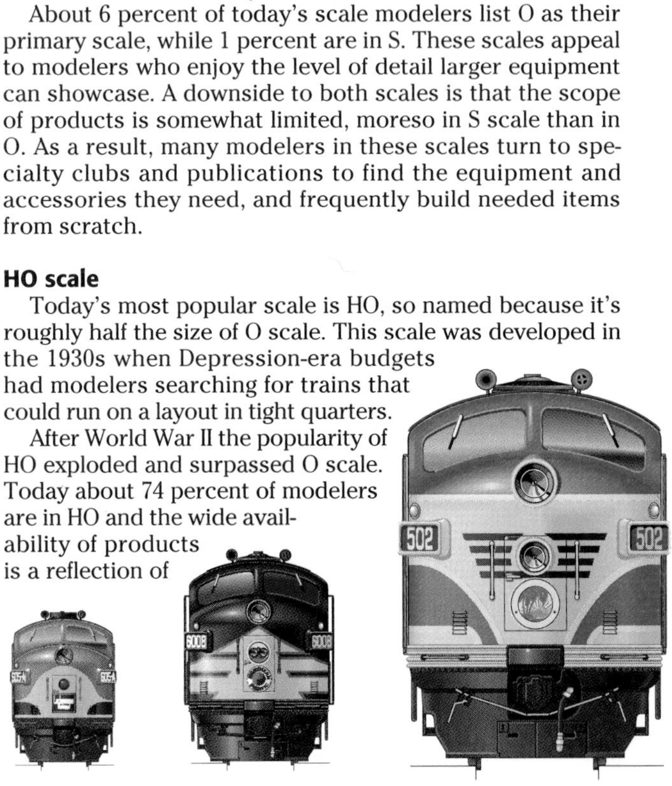

Z scale   N scale   HO scale

the scale's popularity. Wm. K. Walthers, a Milwaukee-based model railroad equipment distributor and manufacturer, each year publishes a catalog of HO equipment that exceeds 850 pages.

Just as Lionel and American Flyer influenced a couple of generations, many of today's model railroaders trace their interest in the hobby to an HO train set they had as a youth. One of HO's biggest advantages is that it can be easily added to and upgraded and basic layouts can be built on a standard sheet of plywood or on a bookshelf.

N scale

N scale emerged in the 1960s and developed in Europe where living quarters tend to be smaller than those in the States. N was given its name because its rails are spaced 9 mm apart and the word for nine begins with "n" in most European languages.

At roughly half the size of HO, you can pack a lot of railroad action in a little bit of space with N scale. About 16 percent of modelers are in N, according to MR surveys, so finding equipment and accessories isn't as difficult as in O or S scales. Most hobby shops have some N scale equipment.

Big G

German manufacturer Lehmann was the pioneer in developing G scale, a large scale proportioned 1:22.5. Lehmann's popular line of LGB trains are actually Gn3 models running on No.1 gauge track. They represent narrow gauge prototypes by using the track gauge of the next smallest scale.

LGB trains are popular among garden railroaders. In fact, G scale took its name from the first letter in "garden" (*garten* in German), as well as from the first letter in the German word for big, *gross*. The American company Bachmann is also a major manufacturer of Gn3 trains, and both brands frequently show up on indoor layouts.

While not G scale, Aristo-Craft trains also run on No. 1 track. They are proportioned 1:29 and represent standard gauge American prototypes. No other manufacturer makes trains to this proportion.

Little Z

Z scale, introduced in 1972, is the new kid on the block and at 1:220 proportion is even smaller than N scale. The German manufacturer Märklin introduced this scale and is

the primary manufacturer. Not needing a lot of space is the key attraction with Z scale. You could build a small layout in a briefcase!

While a lot of Z scale equipment has a European flavor, Micro-Trains Line offers an F7 locomotive and several American prototype cars.

And the rest

There are a couple of other indoor scales you may come across as you make your investigation of scales – OO and TT.

Developed in Europe around the same time HO got its start, OO (1:76) is a bit larger than HO. It's remained almost entirely "Old World" as far as the types of equipment offered.

TT scale, which stands for "table top," first emerged in the late 1950s and was the only scale smaller than HO until N scale came about a decade later. A German company attempted to bring back 1:120 scale in 1993, but went into bankruptcy.

An American company, Railtech, is currently marketing TT track and some European prototype equipment.

Time for decisions

Think you've found a scale and gauge you like? Good, but before you purchase equipment or begin layout benchwork, it might be wise to look at some of the many manuals and handbooks available. Kalmbach offers several books to help HO and N scale modelers. Titles like *HO Model Railroad From Start to Finish*, by MR managing editor Jim Kelly, and *Beginner's Guide to N scale Model Railroading*, by MR publisher Russ Larson, can provide insight to the way things are done in model railroading. See your local hobby dealer for more advice. ✿

S scale

O scale

G scale

What does *that* mean?

No, you don't have to put a duck under your layout

BY MELANIE BUELLESBACH

Here at MODEL RAILROADER we recognize that every month many beginning modelers pick up our magazine for the first time. In our feature stories and departments, we make an effort to explain not-so-common terms that we use. But we can't define every railroad-related term every time, so here's a glossary of some basic model railroad and prototype (real railroad) terms to get you started.

MODEL RAILROAD TERMS

Airbrush: A miniature paint sprayer that will give a controlled application of thinned paint.

Benchwork: A frame which is the foundation of a model railroad layout. L girder and open grid (sometimes called butt-joint) are two popular types (see illustration on opposite page).

CA: Short for cyanoacrylate adhesive, also known as super glue. A high-strength adhesive that can be used on metal and styrene plastic.

Cab control: A method of controlling trains in which one power pack is used for each train so the power pack can be connected to one set of blocks and remain disconnected from all others. A block is an electrically insulated zone of track. Only one engine or set of engines can be controlled in each block.

Command control: A way of controlling trains by sending electronic messages through the rails. Each locomotive has a decoder or receiver which only responds to the messages specifically directed to it. Engines can be controlled independently anywhere on a layout.

Duckunder: An area on a layout where you must bend down and go under the benchwork to gain access to another part of the layout.

Flextrack: Prefabricated flexible sections of track used on a layout. It usually comes in straight, three-foot-long sections which can be bent as needed. Other kinds of track are sectional (rigid pieces of straight and curved track that come with train sets) and handlaid (built with handmade ties, rail, and spikes).

Free-lance: Modeling that does not closely follow a prototype railroad.

Gauge: The distance between the inside of the heads of track rails. Most real railroads in North America and Europe are built to a standard gauge of 4'-8½". Narrow gauge means rails with a width less than standard gauge. For example, On3 means O scale trains with three scale feet between the rails.

Hardshell: A scenery base made by dipping paper towels in plaster and laying them over a light support structure.

Helix: A rising curve which turns around an axis like a corkscrew. Used on multilevel layouts

Scale	Proportion to prototype	Approximate length of 50-foot boxcar
Z	1:220	2¾"
N	1:160	3¾"
HO	1:87	7"
S	1:64	9¼"
O	1:48	12½"
Gn3	1:22.5	19"

Models shown approximately ⅓ actual size

A. L. Schmidt

There are also Z and HO modular societies!

TURNOUT

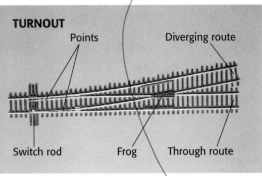

Points
Diverging route
Switch rod
Frog
Through route

to allow trains to go from one level to another.

Homasote: A pressed paperboard often used for roadbed.

Kitbashing: Taking one or more model railroad kits (often structure kits) and changing the construction process or combining parts to make a unique model.

Module: A section of a layout that is built following a standard pattern or dimensions. Each module can be connected interchangeably with any other module built to the same standards. Ntrak is an organization that has developed standards for N scale modules.

Operation: Running trains on a layout in a way that simulates real railroad activity.

Scale: The size of things on a model railroad relative to things on a real railroad (see chart on opposite page). For example, in the most popular scale, HO, models are 1/87th full size.

Scratchbuilding: Making a model from raw materials and parts, not using kits.

Styrene: Short for polystyrene, a versatile plastic commonly used for modeling. Comes in sheets, blocks, and rods of many different thicknesses and sizes.

Turnout: A piece of track that allows a train to go from one track to another (see photo at top of page). Called a switch on a real railroad. Referred to by number. For example, a no. 6 turnout spreads one unit for each six units of travel measured from the frog.

Weathering: Making shiny new models look more realistic by dirtying them up (below).

PROTOTYPE RAILROAD TERMS

Ballast: Layer of crushed rock placed on roadbed to keep track aligned and allow drainage.

Consist: Cars which make up a train; also a list of those cars. Locomotive consist is a group of engines put together to pull a train.

Crossover: Two turnouts and a connecting track that allow a train to be diverted to a parallel track.

Gondola: A long, flat, open car with short sides for hauling items like iron, steel, and scrap.

Hopper car: An open-top car for hauling items that don't need protection like coal and gravel. Unloaded through doors in funnel-like bins in bottom of car. Covered hoppers (right) have roofs; carry grain and other items that need protection from weather.

Intermodal: Shipments that are carried by more than one mode of transportation (below right), mainly containers and piggyback trailers.

MOW: Maintenance-of-way equipment. Used by a railroad to keep track and roadbed in good condition.

Reefer: A refrigerator car. Similar in appearance to a boxcar but has ice or mechanical cooling equipment.

Roadbed: Foundation of built-up earth under tracks.

Rolling stock: Freight and passenger cars.

Running board: Walkway along roof or along sides of tank cars (visible on hopper photo).

Traction: City and suburban trolley lines; equipment run by electricity.

Truck: Assembly holding a group of two or more wheelsets together beneath a car. A wheelset is a pair of wheels connected by an axle.

Uncoupling lever: Also called a cut lever. The device which raises the locking pin in a coupler to allow the knuckle to open for uncoupling.

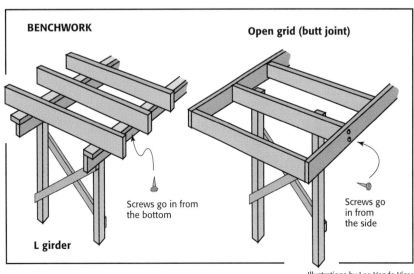

BENCHWORK

Open grid (butt joint)

Screws go in from the bottom

L girder

Screws go in from the side

A modeler's toolbox

Essential tools to make your model railroading more enjoyable

BY JIM HEDIGER
PHOTOS BY THE AUTHOR

Model railroading is a creative hobby that's much more enjoyable if you have the right tools to do the job. Many tools are regular hardware store items, while the more specialized ones are sold by hobby dealers.

Tools come in a wide range of prices, but this is one place where quality is important. Buy the best you can afford, as good tools will perform consistently and with a little care, they'll last a lifetime. Their cheaper cousins tend to be made of softer metals so movable joints loosen and cutting edges wear out much faster.

This list of tools covers the ones most first-time modelers initially acquire. Naturally, there are plenty of other tools available to make more complex projects easier as you gain experience.

The essentials
• **Hobby knife:** The most popular hobby knife has a lightweight knurled aluminum handle with a chuck at one end which holds a sharply-pointed steel blade. You'll also want to pick up some replacement blades. Typical cost is $3 to $5 depending upon the number of extra blades included.
• **Needlenose pliers:** A 6" or 8" needlenose pliers with a built-in wire cutter is useful for everything from adjusting

wheels to spiking track and wiring a layout. A good pair sells for $12 to $15.
• **Screwdrivers:** You'll encounter lots of tiny screws which require small screwdrivers. Look for ones with interchangeable bits or sets with sizes ranging from $\frac{1}{16}$" to $\frac{1}{8}$" plus Phillips sizes 0 and 1. Typical prices range from $5 to $7.50 for single reversible screwdrivers while small sets start around $10.

Useful additions
• **Clamps:** As you build models, you'll find parts must often be held in position while cement dries. A package of spring clothespins from the supermarket is an inexpensive source of clamps. Because they're made of soft wood, the clothespins may be easily trimmed for all sorts of special clamping situations.
• **Mill file:** A single-cut 8" mill file handles truing the edges on plastic kits, smoothing rail joints, and lots of other similar jobs. Don't forget to buy a handle to protect your hand.
• **Needle files:** These small files are about 6" long with extended tang handles and a variety of shapes. They're useful for cleaning flash off castings and filing small openings to exact size. Round and half-round files are the most useful, but sets also include flat, triangular, square, and equaling files. They're sold individually for about $4 or in sets of 6 different shapes for around $20.
• **NMRA gauge:** The National Model Railroad Association produces sheet metal standards gauges for all the popular scales and they're readily available from hobby dealers. One of these gauges makes it easy to check the coupler height and adjust the spacing of wheel sets and track components for top performance. These gauges are $10 each.
• **Paintbrushes:** Watercolor paintbrushes, in sizes 1, 2, and 3, have a lot of uses besides their intended function. Brushes may be used for cleaning and dusting, positioning scenery material, and applying liquid plastic cement. Brush prices start about $2 each.

A small investment in the right tools makes it easier to build and maintain your model railroad.

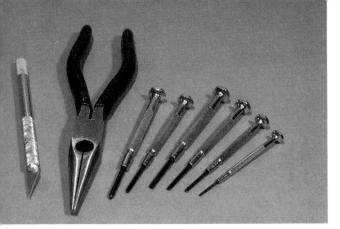

THE ESSENTIALS: Start your toolbox with a hobby knife, a good pair of needlenose pliers, and a set of small screwdrivers.

• **Rail nipper:** This is a special pair of flush-cutting pliers designed to cut soft brass or nickel silver rail in sizes up to code 100. It has a very delicate cutting edge that's easily damaged if you attempt to cut harder materials. Rail nippers sell for about $25 in hobby shops.

• **Soldering iron:** Most modelers learn to solder electrical connections early in the game. A small 30 or 40 watt iron, similar to a wood-burning tool, will do the job for less than $20, while a similar size soldering gun is about $30. You'll also need rosin-core solder with a 60-40 alloy (60 percent tin and 40 percent lead).

• **Tweezers:** Fine-pointed good quality tweezers make it easier to handle small parts. Look for non-magnetic tweezers with perfectly matched machine-ground serrated points (either curved or straight). Misaligned tweezers are useless as the gripping pressure will launch small parts into never-never land. A pair of good tweezers sells for $6 to $10.

Care and handling

Even though they're small, modeling tools require the same care and respect given to their larger counterparts. Think about how much force you're exerting on a small area as you use them. It's easy to damage tiny screws, so use the right size and type of screwdriver and don't overtighten them. Be aware of where the tool is headed if it slips – tiny screwdrivers and hobby knives can inflict some painful wounds.

Hobby knives are extremely sharp, so little pressure is required to make a clean cut. Use a safety cap to prevent accidents when the knife is stored. Blades are inexpensive and dull ones should be replaced for best results. I use a 35mm film can to hold the discarded blades until they can be disposed of safely.

Needle files are hard and brittle, so it doesn't take much side pressure to snap them off. A smooth gentle motion cuts the best. If the file gets stuck in an opening, wiggle it gently in a counter-clockwise circular motion until it comes free. Use a brass suede brush to clean these files. Brush across the file, parallel with the teeth, to clear the debris.

Make sure the surrounding area is clear and wear safety glasses whenever you use rail nippers as the small pieces of rail will go flying as they're cut off. They work best by making two cuts: a rough one to get close and then a final trim that shaves a thin sliver off the end without crushing the rail's cross section.

Finally, soldering creates heat so you need to be careful to let things cool. Some items, like code 100 rail, retain the heat for several seconds after the solder solidifies. (I still have a pair of HO gauge stripes on my forearm from leaning on a track too soon!) Don't forget to disconnect the soldering iron when you're done to eliminate a potential fire hazard.

The important thing is to be patient and let the tools do the work. Forcing a cut or applying undue pressure on anything usually results in disaster. Learn each tool's capabilities and, as you gain experience, you'll find building a model railroad becomes even more enjoyable. ⚙

TWEEZERS AND FILES: Needle files are perfect for cleaning flash out of small openings while the larger mill file does a nice job of finishing rough edges on plastic and metal parts. A good pair of non-magnetic tweezers makes it easy to handle tiny parts.

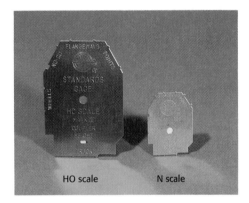

HO scale   N scale

NMRA GAUGE: Get the appropriate gauge for your scale to measure wheels and track spacing as you make adjustments to improve performance.

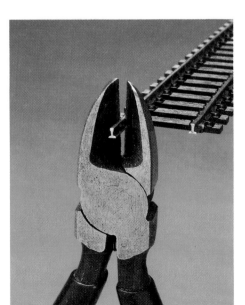

RAIL NIPPERS: These specialized pliers make it easy to cut rail, but safety glasses are a must to protect your eyes from flying bits of rail.

What you need to know about adhesives

Advice and a handy chart to help you choose the right glue for the job

BY GEORGE SEBASTIAN-COLEMAN

ut there in the "real world" things are nailed, screwed, bolted, riveted, and welded together. On our models, though, almost all such connections are made by adhesives – glues. The chart on page 77 shows the qualities of each glue and recommended application. However, I've arranged this article by the material to be joined – metal, wood, plastic – rather than by glue type. After all, we don't sit down in our shops, pick up a tube of glue and say, "What can I build with this?" I'll begin with the toughest materials to glue and work towards the easiest.

Cementing engineering plastics

You can't. Well, that's not quite true, but most plastics which get this label resist gluing. Acetal resins are the type most used in model railroading. They're often referred to as "slippery engineering plastics," the most familiar brand name being Delrin. They're used for trucks, handrails, gears, stirrup steps – anywhere that plastic needs to be very strong or to serve as a bearing.

Small acetal parts can be attached with cyanoacrylate adhesives (CA), but what you're doing is surrounding the part, or a piece of it, with CA, which then holds it in place mechanically. You can similarly glue pieces made from Teflon, nylon, and other engineering plastics, but all of these joints will be very weak.

Joining metal

Epoxy resins can bond metal to metal with almost the strength of solder. For most people the main advantage of epoxy over solder is the ability to reposition parts, as it takes 5 to 20 minutes to cure. But this setting time can be a drawback as the pieces must be held in position for that long. Epoxy also works well for joining metal to virtually any other material.

Cyanoacrylate adhesives (CAs, also called super glues) are excellent for joining metal to metal and metal to almost anything else. The thin CAs produce the quickest and strongest joints, but the joint must be very close-fitting. The best approach is to assemble the pieces then just touch the CA to the joint and let capillary action draw it in – the less glue the better. The thicker, or "gap-filling," CAs do not require snug joints. These should also be used when gluing metal to porous substances such as wood or cardstock.

General purpose glues, such as those made by Ambroid and Duco, can also be used for low-stress metal joints, like adding weights to rolling stock. Sometimes their fumes can attack plastics, so try double-sided foam tape instead. It's easy to use and won't harm a thing.

Welding styrene

Styrene is the most common plastic in model kits. It's cheap, easy to cast, and more than strong enough for most parts. It's also incredibly easy to glue. The adhesives we think of as "plastic cements" are actually solvents. They dissolve a layer of plastic on each piece and weld the two together. Besides all the brand name glues, you can also use methyl-ethyl-ketone (MEK) available at hardware stores.

Like CAs, plastic glues vary in thickness. On the

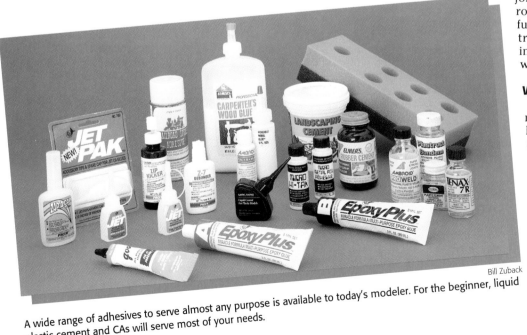

Bill Zuback

A wide range of adhesives to serve almost any purpose is available to today's modeler. For the beginner, liquid plastic cement and CAs will serve most of your needs.

Adhesive	Setting time	Curing time	Strength	Color	Best applications
Cyanoacrylate	5 - 60 sec.	2 hrs.	high	clear	metal, plastic, wood
Contact cement	on contact	24 hrs.	medium	light brown	cardstock, plastic, Styrofoam, wood
Epoxy	5 - 20 min.	12 hrs.	high	clear, amber	cardstock, metal, plastic, wood
General purpose	10 - 20 min.	12 hrs.	medium	clear, amber	cardboard, metal, styrene, wood
Plastic cement	30 sec. - 1 min.	8 hrs.	medium	clear	styrene
White glue	10 - 60 min.	24 hrs.	high	clear	cardstock, plaster, scenery, wood
Yellow glue	10 - 40 min.	24 hrs.	high	clear	cardstock, plaster, Styrofoam, wood

thin side, but arranged in increasing viscosity, they are MEK, Tenax 7R, Testor's liquid plastic cement, and Plastruct's Plastic Weld. "Airplane glue" is at the gel end of the scale.

The thin cements work very well and produce almost invisible joints on tight-fitting seams. However, as with CAs, you may find the thicker ones more useful when gluing parts that don't mate closely. Testor's "Model Master Liquid Plastic Cement" is thicker than most and has a needle-tube applicator allowing you to apply a precise amount. This gives you the slow setting time needed to position parts and still have neat joints.

There's no advantage to using CAs for styrene-to-styrene joints, but they will work. For gluing styrene to other materials, CAs are usually the preferred choice. However, general purpose glues, such as those made by Ambroid or Duco, will usually provide a satisfactory bond. Contact cements (Walthers Goo is one; there are many others including spray-on types) will give the best results when gluing sheets of plastic, such as brick sheets, to one another or to some other material.

Gluing wood, cardstock, and plaster

These are perhaps the easiest items to glue because they are porous. However, many adhesives won't work on them. The very thin CAs generally won't work, nor will the plastic cements. The most useful glues for joining one porous material to another are the familiar white glues, such as Elmer's Glue-All, and yellow glues like Titebond's Carpenter's Wood Glue. Both clean up in water, but the yellow glues will resist dissolving in water once set. You can also thin both with water, but this greatly reduces their strength and should only be done when you want the glue to soak deeply into a material, track ballast for example.

As they were for styrene, contact cements are the choice for gluing large sheets of wood or paper together. Contact cements are applied to each surface, allowed to partially set, then the two parts are pressed together. Because this joint is permanent, you must be careful to align the parts correctly the first time.

Scenery glues

The most common bonding challenge in scenery is joining a loose accumulation of ground cover or ballast into a solid unit. You can use thinned white glue for this purpose, but it can leave an unrealistic sheen. Acrylic matte medium – available at art stores – will provide a good bond yet leave the ground looking dry. Several manufacturers offer their own version of this material, such as Life-Like's Landscaping Cement.

Heun Enterprise's Moveable Model Glue and Ambroid's Hob-E-Tac are two more variations on white glue. These glues remain tacky so you can remove a part and then replace it. I've also found them very good for adding glazing to windows.

Spray adhesives, such as Floquil's "All Purpose Scenery Spray Adhesive" can be used to affix ground-foam foliage to trees or as a bond for ground cover. It also functions as a spray-on contact cement. Cheap hair spray, the cheaper the better, also works well for attaching ground foam to tree trunks.

Styrofoam insulation can be glued with white glues by applying a thin coat to both pieces, letting them dry a bit, and pressing together. You can also use construction glues – Liquid Nails is the best known. You should test these first as some brands have solvents which may attack the plastic – don't worry if they eat in a little, as long as they hold. Construction glues are also excellent for putting up backdrops and adding fascia to the front of the layout.

Safety

Many adhesives or their fumes can irritate your skin, eyes, and the membranes in your nose and mouth. All vapors should be considered potentially toxic. Work in a well-ventilated area, and take frequent breaks. Stop immediately if you feel dizzy. The most hazardous adhesives are CAs because they can instantly glue skin to itself and anything else. Acetone, nail polish remover, and special debonding agents can help free you. Should you get some in your eye or another sensitive area get medical attention immediately – do not pry apart! A foam bottle holder, like that in the photo, will keep CA bottles and other glues and paints from spilling and ruining you or your models.

Sticking to the subject

There are other glues out there and with the daily advances in material engineering you can be sure there will be new ones soon. The best way to discover what works for you is to try them all. The glue one person swears by may be the one you only swear at. With all the choices, however, you should be able to make almost anything stick together. ⍥

Flextrack for smooth operation

A little care and patience pays big dividends

BY JIM HEDIGER

Building reliable model railroad track doesn't take a lot of expertise or fancy tools, but it does require care and patience.

Train sets traditionally include an oval of sectional track that's fine for getting a quick start. However, most modelers choose flextrack when they begin building a permanent layout. It's supplied in 36-inch or meter lengths that can be cut to length and bent to the radius desired.

Track materials

Track is sold in a number of sizes, called "codes," which indicate the rail height in thousandths of an inch. Code 100 (.100"), code 83 (.083"), and code 70 (.070") are common sizes in HO scale while code 80, code 70, and code 55 are used for N scale. These sizes represent the various sizes real railroads use as shown in fig. 1.

You'll also be faced with choosing brass, nickel-silver, or steel rail. At one time nearly all HO track was made with brass rail. However, the yellow color isn't realistic and brass must be kept quite clean for efficient electrical contact. Nickel silver is a similar soft-metal rail with a more realistic silver-gray color and better electrical conductivity. Steel rail is used in Bachmann's flextrack and its color is perfect, but the rails are difficult to cut and file.

Small flat metal sleeves called rail joiners are used to connect sections of scale track. Molded plastic rail joiners are used for electrically insulated joints.

Smooth foundation

Good track requires a smooth foundation, so ½" or ¾" plywood is the proven choice here. Use the five-ply exterior grade with plugged and machine sanded surfaces. This grade has five veneer layers held together with waterproof resin glue to resist warping and moisture; it won't be affected by water when you begin scenery construction.

An electric saber saw does a fine job of cutting track boards. Remember to allow enough width along each side of the roadbed to attach scenery materials. In HO use a minimum 3" width for single track or 6" for a double track. Half these sizes works well for N scale. Use a solid sheet under the yards and town areas.

Splices in the track boards deserve special attention or you'll have difficulty laying track over them. See fig. 2.

Lay out and mark the track center lines and then install the roadbed. In critical areas, it's best to fit the track components together first and then mark the appropriate center lines between the ties. Allow more space between curved track centers to provide clearance between trains on adjacent tracks.

Cork is the most popular roadbed and it's sold in 36-inch lengths. Each length has a 45-degree split down the middle so it can be separated easily. Tack the roadbed halves down with ½" wire nails to produce the ballast cross section. Take care to stagger the roadbed joints so they don't fall directly over the track board joints. Use a sharp hobby knife to trim the cork and a Stanley

Trains glide realistically through the smooth-flowing curves any modeler can build with commercial flextrack.

Fig. 1 RAIL SIZES

	Code 100	Code 83	Code 70
Prototype equivalent for HO scale	156 pounds per yard	132 pounds per yard	100 pounds per yard
Typical use	Heaviest main lines (rare)	Typical main line	Secondary routes and sidings

	Code 80	Code 70	Code 55
Prototype equivalent for N scale	227 pounds per yard (45 percent oversize)	198 pounds per yard (27 percent oversize)	156 pounds per yard
Typical use	Heavy main lines	Heavy main lines	Heavy main lines

Surform block plane to smooth the joints and shape the ballast.

Tracklaying

Once the foundation is ready, it's time to begin laying the track. Start at a group of switches or a crossing where several different track alignments come together and then work out in all directions, blending the approach tracks as smoothly as possible.

Most track components are made with spike holes next to the rails. Some brands also have small depressions cored into the underside of the plastic ties so you may use a small drill to easily open a few extra holes to secure the track exactly as you want it. Use long-nose pliers to drive the spikes as shown in fig. 3.

As you join the track sections, lean down and sight along the rails to check the alignment at the joints.

Test-fit each track section and trim it to fit. You can cut rail with a fine-tooth razor saw, a cut-off disk in a motor tool, or a pair of rail nippers. The rail nippers are the quickest of the three, but be sure to wear safety glasses.

Cutting leaves a small burr that interferes with the rail joiner slipping on easily. Smooth the cut rail ends with a file before you add the joiners. You may also need to notch or remove a couple of ties to clear the joiner.

Soldering rail joints

Spike the track section leading into the curve, but let the last few inches straighten out. Slip the next section into the rail joiners, carefully align the rails, and then solder both joints. After the joint cools, bend the flextrack and continue spiking around the curve. Trim off the inside rail before you make the next joint. Use a small jeweler's file to remove any excess solder and smooth the tops and insides of the railheads.

The wood in most layouts expands and contracts with seasonal changes in temperature and humidity while the rails remain static. If all the joints are soldered, the rails will kink as the wood drys out and shrinks during the heating season. On my Ohio Southern RR, I solder the joints on curves but rely on the normal mechanical joints in the straightaways. As I lay these straight sections, I use the metal rail joiners for alignment but leave a .020" gap between the rail ends. Temporarily slipping a small piece of .020" styrene between the rail ends will maintain the gap while you spike down the track. These small gaps allow the track to shift a little to prevent kinking as the layout contracts.

Within reach

Thanks to our commercial suppliers, good track is now within the reach of every model railroader. Start slowly and deliberately, taking care to get things right the first time. Remember, you're creating a smooth path for your trains to follow. With patience and practice, you'll find tracklaying is fun. ✿

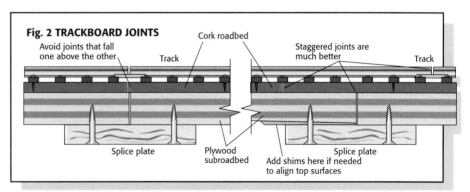

Fig. 2 TRACKBOARD JOINTS
Avoid joints that fall one above the other
Cork roadbed
Track
Staggered joints are much better
Track
Splice plate
Plywood subroadbed
Add shims here if needed to align top surfaces
Splice plate

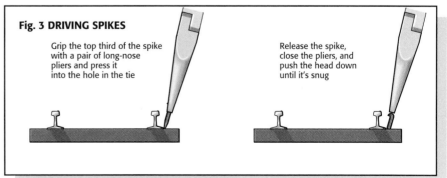

Fig. 3 DRIVING SPIKES
Grip the top third of the spike with a pair of long-nose pliers and press it into the hole in the tie
Release the spike, close the pliers, and push the head down until it's snug

All about turnouts

Terminology, types, and troubleshooting

BY JIM HEDIGER
PHOTOS BY JIM FORBES

Turnouts route our trains and provide access to other tracks. Without them our models would be doomed to run along one track forever, so let's take a closer look.

Many newcomers and experienced railroaders refer to turnouts as switches, but that term is easily confused with electrical switches used in model railroad wiring. In engineering terms a "switch" is only the moving point rails, while a "turnout" is the entire unit.

Terminology

While they come in a variety of sizes, most turnouts are similar in construction. Figure 1 shows an example with the names of the various parts that we'll be referring to from here on.

Prototype and model turnout sizes are expressed as a number which indicates the angle of the "frog" where the tracks diverge. These numbers are shorthand for the length to width ratio of the diverging angle, so a no. 4 turnout takes four inches to spread one inch, a no. 6 takes six inches to reach the one-inch spread, and so on. I've used inches here, but the turnout frog number remains the same with any linear measurements. The higher the number, the gentler the angle through the turnout.

Because of layout space constraints, modelers tend to use mostly no. 4s and no. 5s in yards and industrial spurs and no. 6s for main lines. No. 8s appear in large layouts that operate long-wheelbase steam locomotives and

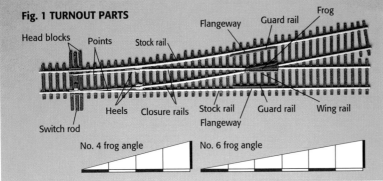

Fig. 1 TURNOUT PARTS

Head blocks · Points · Stock rail · Flangeway · Guard rail · Frog · Heels · Closure rails · Stock rail · Guard rail · Wing rail · Switch rod · Flangeway

No. 4 frog angle   No. 6 frog angle

Illustrations by Robert Wegner

Fig. 2 TURNOUT CONSTRUCTION. This low angle view shows the difference between the diverging routes in a regular numbered turnout (no. 6) on the left and one designed to fit into an 18"-radius train set curve.

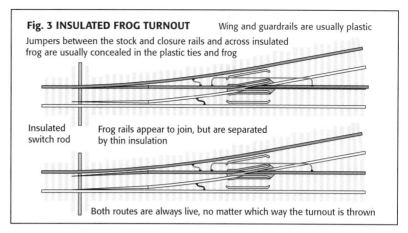

Fig. 3 INSULATED FROG TURNOUT Wing and guardrails are usually plastic

Jumpers between the stock and closure rails and across insulated frog are usually concealed in the plastic ties and frog

Insulated switch rod

Frog rails appear to join, but are separated by thin insulation

Both routes are always live, no matter which way the turnout is thrown

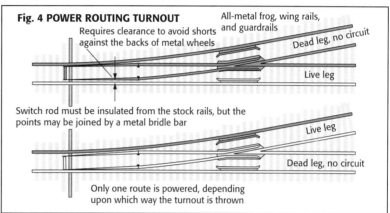

Fig. 4 POWER ROUTING TURNOUT All-metal frog, wing rails, and guardrails

Requires clearance to avoid shorts against the backs of metal wheels

Dead leg, no circuit

Live leg

Switch rod must be insulated from the stock rails, but the points may be joined by a metal bridle bar

Live leg

Dead leg, no circuit

Only one route is powered, depending upon which way the turnout is thrown

full-length passenger cars. All of these sizes are extremely sharp compared to prototype practices where a no. 8 is considered sharp and most mainline turnouts are in the no. 12 to no. 20 range.

The turnout size is what determines the maximum running speed allowed through the diverging route. A good rule of thumb here is the speed limit is twice the frog number: 8 mph for a no. 4 or 12 mph for a no. 6. That's why modelers have difficulty keeping trains on the track as they race through a no. 6 switch at a scale 80 mph!

Curved or angled?

Turnouts made for train set use by Atlas, Bachmann, Life-Like, and Model Power have diverging routes which are curved from their points, through the frog, and beyond to match 18"-radius curved track. See fig. 2. In most cases, these turnouts can be substituted for any full section of curved or straight track in a layout just like toy train switches.

Numbered turnouts have a slight curve through the points and closure rails, but their rails straighten out through and beyond the frog as shown in fig. 2.

Electrical characteristics

Turnouts have different electrical characteristics depending on whether they're made with insulated or solid frogs. A molded plastic frog and insulated switch rod are the tip-offs that the turnout is insulated and has built-in jumpers to power all of the rails with the proper polarity at all times. These turnouts make wiring a small layout easy because only two electrical feeder wires are required. See fig. 3.

An all-metal frog indicates a power routing turnout. Here the position of the points determines which route is powered for a train to run. See fig. 4. Insulated rail joiners are required to prevent shorts when turnouts are placed frog to frog and if a power feeder is attached beyond the frog, but the selective power routing feature is handy for yard and industrial spur tracks. Chapter 3 in Andy Sperandeo's book *Your Guide to Easy Model Railroad Wiring*, published by Kalmbach, includes more detailed explanations of these situations.

Most experienced modelers prefer the power routing feature of the selective turnouts. Their solid frogs also provide better electrical pickup for locomotives with short wheelbases.

Troubleshooting

Careful attention to detail is important when installing turnouts, as they have several potential derailment points. Try to create as smooth a path as possible for the wheels. Use a small jeweler's file to smooth and sharpen each switchpoint. Then slide a fingernail along the inside of the railhead to make sure there's a smooth transition for the wheels to follow between the stock rail and the point. If your nail catches, the wheels will too.

Next, smooth the joints between the heels of the points and the closure rails. Then make sure the frog and its guardrails are free of flash or excess solder. You may also want to sharpen the frog point so the wheels slide off instead of striking it.

A National Model Railroad Association standards gauge is handy to have if you run into derailment problems. These sheet metal gauges are made for all scales, and they're sold in most hobby shops. Each gauge has a number of pins and notches to measure a variety of critical turnout and wheelset dimensions as shown in fig. 5. An instruction sheet is provided that explains each function.

The last step is to roll a car through the switch. Listen and watch closely as it passes over the areas listed above. Any loud clicks or sudden lurches indicate a problem. If the car rolls though unimpeded, you're ready to get on with running trains. ⚙

Fig. 5 NMRA GAUGE. These steel gauges allow modelers to easily check track components for conformance with the National Model Railroad Association's standards.

Hide those switch motors

Concealed mounting techniques to improve your layout's appearance

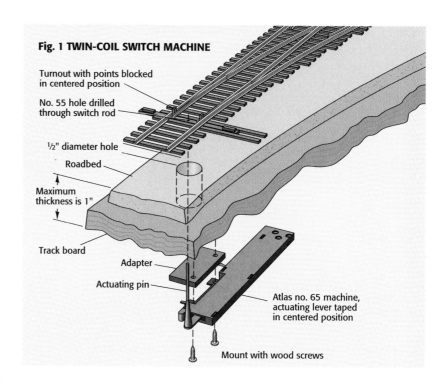

Fig. 1 TWIN-COIL SWITCH MACHINE

Turnout with points blocked in centered position

No. 55 hole drilled through switch rod

1/2" diameter hole

Roadbed

Maximum thickness is 1"

Track board

Adapter

Actuating pin

Atlas no. 65 machine, actuating lever taped in centered position

Mount with wood screws

BY JIM HEDIGER

odel railroaders often use powered turnouts to route trains at the push of a button. Unfortunately, most model switch machines don't look anything like the real thing and are huge in proportion to the track. That's why many modelers prefer to hide them under the layout.

Electrically operated switch machines fall into two categories based on how they work. The first type is a twin-coil solenoid with a movable core that's instantly attracted to an energized coil at either end of its travel. The other is a geared motor that takes several seconds to move the switch points.

Twin-coil machines

Ads for twin-coil switch machines date back to MODEL RAILROADER's earliest issues in 1934. The machines' operating principle remains the same, although today's machines are considerably smaller than those early ones.

The Atlas no. 65 bottom-mounting switch machine is a popular twin-coil unit that's easy to install. It has a black plastic case with a molded actuating lever and is designed to mount flush against the underside of your track board. However, the combined thickness of the

track board and roadbed cannot exceed 1 inch. The machine must also be mounted level and parallel to the turnout it operates.

Figure 1 shows how all the components fit together above and below the track board. It's best to lay the track up to the turnout so you know the exact location of the switch rod. Use tiny bits of wood to block the points in a centered position between the outside rails, then drill a no. 55 pilot hole down through the switch rod, roadbed, and track board. Remove the switch and enlarge the hole through the roadbed and track board to 1/2". Smooth any rough edges with a round file or a rolled-up piece of sandpaper.

Position the machine's small manual operating lever at the center of its travel and add bits of masking tape to hold it there. This allows you to handle the switch machine without disturbing its mid-travel position.

Slip the actuating pin up through the large opening beneath the switch so it enters the smaller hole in the switch rod. Add the spacing adapter and install one screw to secure the machine to the underside of the trackboard. Remove the tape and blocking and manually throw the switch to test the movement of the

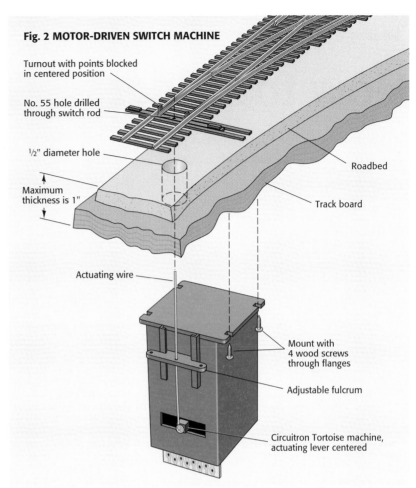

Fig. 2 MOTOR-DRIVEN SWITCH MACHINE

Turnout with points blocked
in centered position

No. 55 hole drilled
through switch rod

½" diameter hole

Maximum
thickness is 1"

Roadbed

Track board

Actuating wire

Mount with
4 wood screws
through flanges

Adjustable fulcrum

Circuitron Tortoise machine,
actuating lever centered

Illustrations by Rick Johnson

Bill Zuback

A thin wire extending up through the center of the switch rod is the only visible part of the concealed switch machine.

points. The throw can be adjusted by gently sliding the machine one way or the other, using the mounting screw as a fulcrum. When the point action is even, add the second mounting screw.

Connect the wiring according to the manufacturer's instructions.

Motor-driven machines

Geared, motor-driven switch machines became popular in the mid-1980s as modelers discovered the realism of their slow motion. These machines are also easier on the track switch as the points move gently rather than slamming hard against the stock rails. The Circuitron Tortoise machine is a typical example.

Here, a small motor drives a gear-driven mechanism that throws the switch points, taking a second or two to move from one position to the other. The motor draws a maximum of only 15 milliamperes of DC current, so it can safely stall at the end of its travel and remain stalled under power without damage. Reversing the polarity changes the direction of its motion.

The Tortoise also mounts directly under the switch points as shown in fig. 2. Here again, a hole must be drilled through the track board and roadbed to provide clearance for the actuating wire. Once the location of the switch rod has been determined, the mounting hole locations can be easily marked using a template printed on the Circuitron instruction sheet. Then four screws are used to attach the machine to the track board.

The adjustable fulcrum is a handy feature on the Tortoise machine. It can be shifted up or down to change the tension on the switch points and adjust the length of throw to operate turnouts in any scale.

Circuitron's instruction sheet shows several different wiring methods. It also explains how the machine's built-in double-pole double-throw electrical contacts can be used to control trackside signals or position indicators on a control panel.

Turnout control wiring

All of the manufacturers include basic wiring diagrams in their instructions, but they only cover operation of one machine at a time. If you're building a yard or junction, I'd recommend reading chapter 9 of Andy Sperandeo's book, *Easy Model Railroad Wiring* (Kalmbach Publishing Co.), to find out more about controlling groups of switch machines. ◊

How to solder

Soldered wire connections are a must for good electrical contact

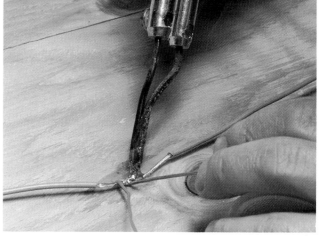

Jim Forbes

This simple Tee splice connects wires under a layout.

BY GEORGE SEBASTIAN-COLEMAN

Soldering may not be necessary to build fine-looking locomotives for your layout, but if you want them to move you still need to master the basics of soldering wire connections.

How solder works

Solder joins metals together by creating a molecular bond between itself and the various pieces to be joined.

To accomplish this the metals to be joined must first be heated enough that the solder melts when it touches them. Merely putting molten solder on a joint won't produce a strong bond, if it produces a bond at all.

The second requirement for a good bond is that the surfaces be clean, that is bare metal, free of oxides or dirt and grease.

The secret

There isn't one. You simply put the two ideas I've just explained into practice – clean surfaces sufficiently heated.

Getting heat

There are lots of ways to heat the parts you want to join, but the most common for wiring, and happily the least expensive, is the electric soldering iron, see fig. 1. These are available in a variety of wattages – some are even adjustable. The higher the wattage the more heat available.

For most wiring applications a 40-watt iron will be plenty. For working around electronics a 25-watt iron may be more convenient. With its trigger on-off feature, you may find a soldering gun useful for working under the layout and with larger diameter wires or parts.

Just as the metal to be joined needs to be clean, so does the tip of the soldering iron. File the tip clean, coat it with flux (a liquid or paste which prevents oxidation of the metal while it's being heated), melt some solder onto it, and then wipe the solder off with a damp rag. Keep a damp sponge near your work area and wipe the tip on it after each use to keep it bright. A bright tip will transfer heat more quickly.

Cleaning up

Wire which has been freshly stripped of its insulation shouldn't require any cleaning beyond the use of flux. Wire or brass pieces that are dirty or oxidized will require some abrasive cleaning. Sandpaper, steel wool, files, or just scraping with a knife can all be used to clean a metal surface. Clean the metal just before you solder. Once you have a shiny surface, apply some flux.

Flux comes in many forms, but the most common and useful for wiring is liquid rosin flux in a squeeze bottle. Drops of flux can be squeezed directly onto the joint or you can make a small puddle on your work surface and use a brush to apply it. See fig. 2 for soldering a wire splice.

Never use acid flux on electrical connections. Indeed you really shouldn't need anything but rosin flux for most model railroad applications.

Fig. 1 SOLDERING SUPPLIES. A soldering stand safely holds the hot iron; this one also has a sponge to keep the tip clean. Liquid rosin flux and .025"-diameter rosin-core solder are excellent choices for model work. Heat-shrink tubing makes neater and smaller joints than electrical tape.

George Sebastian-Coleman

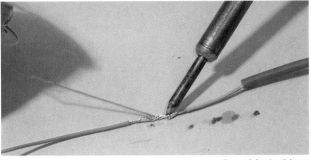

Fig. 2 A Western Union splice is the preferred choice for end-to-end connections. Note the heat-shrink tubing to the right.

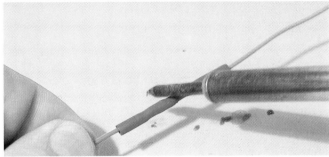

The heat-shrink tubing has been slipped over the joint and is being shrunk tight by rubbing the warm side of the iron – not the hot tip – on all sides.

Making connections

Several recommended ways to splice two wires are shown in fig. 3. In most cases you can make your splice, apply flux, then heat and add solder. However, if it's difficult to support the wires, it's best to tin each wire – lightly coat it with solder – before making the splice.

To tin your wire, strip away the insulation, put some flux on the exposed wire, touch the iron to the end of the wire, and apply solder near the insulation. The solder will melt and flow toward the tip.

Now when you make your splice you probably won't need any additional solder, so you'll be able to support the wire with your free hand. The drawback to this method is that the tinned wires are more difficult to wrap around each other.

Soldering electrical feeders to rail follows the same basic steps as a wire to wire connection. Some additional tips are shown in fig. 4.

Use plenty of heat so the solder melts quickly. This will keep the ties from melting. Also, you don't want to disturb a solder joint as it cools so don't use the iron to hold the wire in place.

Other projects

Once you've gained confidence with these simple connections you'll realize soldering is not hard and want to do more. Just remember, the requirements for a good joint don't change regardless of technique or material: You always need clean surfaces sufficiently heated. ⚙

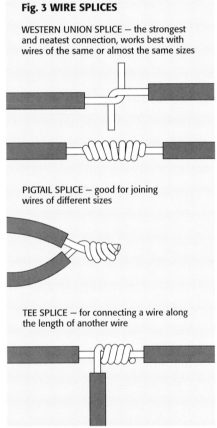

Fig. 3 WIRE SPLICES

WESTERN UNION SPLICE – the strongest and neatest connection, works best with wires of the same or almost the same sizes

PIGTAIL SPLICE – good for joining wires of different sizes

TEE SPLICE – for connecting a wire along the length of another wire

Illustration by Rick Johnson

Fig. 4 TRACK FEEDERS.
Left: After inserting the feeder through the roadbed, put a 90-degree bend in it and tin. **Middle**: Scrape away any weathering or corrosion on the rail, then flux and tin it. Now bend the feeder so it rests against the web of the rail under the head. **Right:** You can use an aluminum soldering tool to hold the feeder in place as you apply heat. Be sure your iron is hot so the solder melts quickly.

Cab control

Simple wiring for two trains

BY ANDY SPERANDEO

Running one train is fun, as a new model railroader quickly discovers. It's natural, then, to go for twice as much fun by running two trains.

However, we can't just set another train on the same loop or line of track and control it independently. Both locomotives will respond to the electricity delivered through the rails by the power pack, and so will move in the same direction at roughly the same speed. For independent control we need a way to connect each locomotive to a separate power pack through different parts of the track, and that's cab control.

Blocks and switches

In cab control we divide the track into several insulated, electrically isolated sections called "blocks." Each block has its own power wires or "feeders" connected to an electrical switch on the layout's control panel. We use the switch to connect the block to one or the other of two "cabs." (A cab can be a single power pack, one half of a twin power pack, or even a locomotive sound system.) Figure 1 shows cab control wiring for a single block.

By switching the blocks from cab to cab as the trains move around the layout, we can control each train independently. The switch used as the cab selector is a "double-throw" type – it throws one way or the other – so only one cab at a time can be connected to a block. The only way to get into trouble is to run a train across the insulation into a block connected to the other cab. That means the engineer has to pay attention, and that's not a bad idea anyway.

Layout wiring

In fig. 2 you see all the cab control wiring for a simple layout. It might look complicated, but it's just a repetitive pattern based on the arrangement in fig. 1. Once you see how this

---

A cab control glossary

Block: a section of electrically isolated track with its own power connection ("feeder") and cab selector switch.

Cab: the speed and direction controller for one train.

Common rail: an electrically continuous rail running throughout a layout and connected directly to both cabs. The opposite rail, the "controlled rail," is the only one that needs insulation to define blocks and feeders connected through the cab selector switches.

(If you're not familiar with electrical circuits, the common connection between power packs in fig. 2 may look like trouble. It's not, though, because electricity only flows where there's a complete circuit out from the power supply, through the engine's motor, and back to the same supply.)

Feeder: a wire connected to a rail to feed power to the train. Feeder connections can be made with standard terminal track sections, but it's helpful to know a couple of other methods that allow more flexibility. In HO and N scales there's the option of using terminal joiners, metal rail joiners you can buy with feeder wires already soldered in place. Just use these in place of the regular metal joiners to make connections at any rail joint. Most experienced modelers learn to solder wires directly to the rail

so they can put feeders wherever they need them. *Easy Model Railroad Wiring* shows you how.

Plastic rail joiner: a rail connection made of insulating plastic that takes the place of a metal joiner to divide the controlled rail into blocks. Another way is to cut a gap in the rail with a saw or an abrasive wheel in a motor tool. It's a good idea to fill the gap with wood or plastic to keep the rails from creeping back together and making an unwanted connection.

Single-pole, double-throw switch (abbreviated SPDT): a switch that can connect one wire, the moving "pole," to either of two other wires. Any kind of switch – slide, toggle,

or rotary – fitting this description can be used for cab control.

Another useful feature for selector switches is a "center off" position. This allows a block to be completely off and not connected to either cab, which is handy for parking a train or locomotive. If track space allows, you can have several trains or engines on the layout as long as you run no more than two at a time.

The Atlas Selector: a control-panel unit with four SPDT center-off slide switches and easy-to-use screw connections for cab control with two cabs and four blocks. Any number of Selectors can be ganged together to control a larger number of blocks.

Fig. 1 BASIC CAB CONTROL

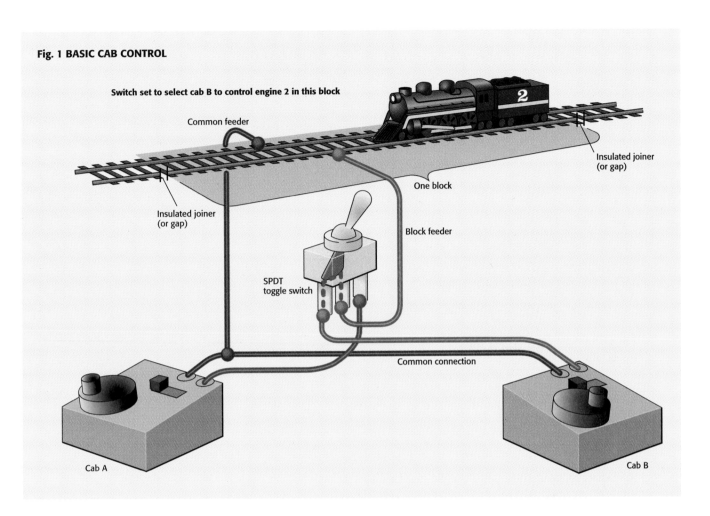

Switch set to select cab B to control engine 2 in this block

Common feeder

Insulated joiner
(or gap)

One block

Insulated joiner
(or gap)

Block feeder

SPDT
toggle switch

Common connection

Cab A

Cab B

works, you can apply cab control wiring to a layout of any size.

As you run a train around the layout, you flip the switch for the next block ahead to your cab, so your train stays connected to your cab. Your buddy the other engineer does the same thing, and the two of you can operate independently as long as you keep both trains from entering the same block.

Where do you get the stuff you need to wire a layout for cab control? Try your hobby shop first, but not all hobby shops carry a wide range of wiring supplies. You may need to learn your way around a Radio Shack store or an electrical supply dealer (see your *Yellow Pages*). You'll also find several electrical suppliers advertising in MODEL RAILROADER, so you can get what you need by mail.

If you're thinking there must be more to it than this, you're absolutely right. In my book, *Easy Model Railroad Wiring*, three of the twelve chapters develop and expand on the concept of cab control. Look for it at your hobby store, or call us, Kalmbach Publishing, at 1-800-533-6644 if you can't find it.

The core idea, though, is this simple, and you'll find you can do a lot of railroading with basic cab control. ☼

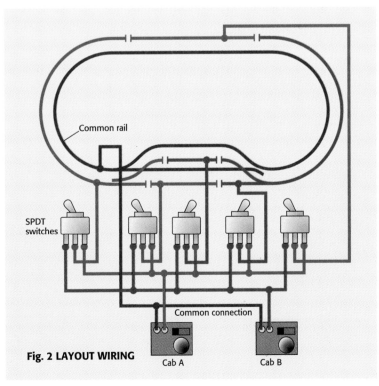

Common rail

SPDT
switches

Common connection

Cab A

Cab B

Fig. 2 LAYOUT WIRING

DCC: what it is and what it does

A control system that runs your trains, rather than your tracks

BY JIM KELLY

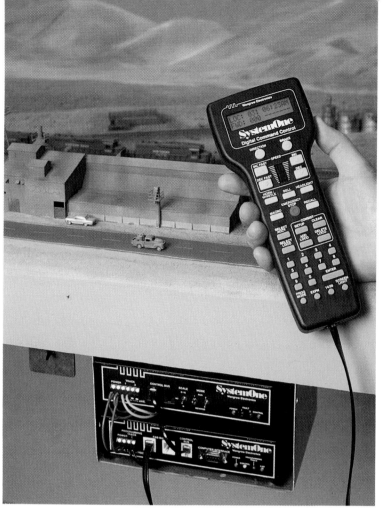

Photos by Rebecca Saliture

Author Jim Kelly runs his small N scale layout with Wangrow's System One. The command station and power booster are in separate boxes, seen here stacked on a bracket under this Ntrak module. The display on the walkaround throttle guides the user through programming and operating steps.

While reading through this magazine or looking at the ads you're going to see the letters DCC. They stand for Digital Command Control, a means of controlling electrical devices that conforms to a set of standards approved by the NMRA (National Model Railroad Association).

Knowing what those letters stand for isn't any help, though, unless you know what command control is. It's a means of controlling electrical devices by sending electronic messages through the rails. Think of it as like radio, except that radio waves travel through the air.

The electrical devices we're most interested in controlling are the motors inside locomotives.

Here's why: Consider fig. 1, which illustrates how model trains are controlled by a conventional DC power pack. In a single electrical block we can run only one engine, or group of engines, at a time. Real locomotives are under no such constraints and can run right up to each other. The engineer is in control, not some outside power source.

Decoders and black boxes

One way to achieve independence for our locomotives is to put the means of controlling the motor inside the engine itself. See fig. 2. Enter the command control system, which includes several components.

Let's start with the locomotive. Inside is a very smart electrical device which responds only to signals that are meant specifically for it. In DCC systems this device is called a decoder. There's power on the rails at all times, but the train won't go until the decoder tells it to.

The messages the decoder receives are generated inside a black box called a command station. As created, the control signals are weak, and so a second black box, called a power booster, is needed to amplify them and pump them out through the rails. Thousands of these little messages (called packets) can be sent in a second. The booster also supplies the power to

Here's a System One N scale decoder installed in one of the author's Atlas GP30s. To make room for the decoder, Jim swapped out the stock frame for a milled one from Aztec.

the track, a constant 12-14 volts AC, which the engines draw upon once they're asked to run.

Power for both these black boxes is provided by a transformer which reduces the 110-volt AC current in your house wiring to a more manageable and safer level, usually around 18 volts. (In some systems all these components are packaged together in one cabinet.)

Putting you in charge

We need one more component to complete a system, and that's a means for telling the command station what we'd like it to do. In most systems this is a handheld throttle, and with most layouts you'll want two or more, enough for everyone who's running trains at the same time.

With most systems, at least one throttle serves double-duty. It's also used to program the decoders, and the most important part of that job is assigning them their electronic addresses. A new decoder comes already assigned address 3. The customary procedure is to install it, then re-address it to the locomotive's road number. This takes only a minute or two and is done with the command station switched to its programming mode and the engine sitting on a programming track electrically isolated from the rest of the railroad.

While you're programming the engine you can also do other things, such as assign minimum starting voltage and adjust rates of acceleration and deceleration. Fortunately you don't have to do any of these things if you don't want to. The manufacturers' default settings work very well.

A DCC system allows you not only to run an engine, but also to turn lights on and off, blow whistles, ring bells, and more. You can also control off-train devices such as turnouts. The circuits that perform these feats are called "func-

tions," and some systems have as many as nine.

Consisting (running a group of engines together on one throttle) is a matter of telling the system that's what you want it to do and entering the engine numbers. You can add engines to an existing consist or delete the whole consist or just part of it whenever you want.

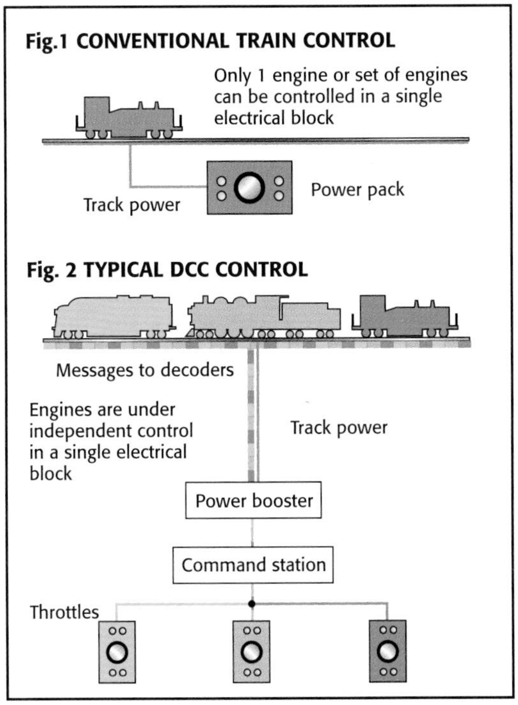

A long row to hoe

Command control is an extremely realistic way to run trains, yet probably fewer than 10 percent of our readers use it. The reasons are easy to understand:

• Expense. Getting into even the least expensive systems will cost upwards of $500.

• Difficulty. Hooking up a command control system is fairly easy, but installing decoders in locomotives can be a considerable challenge, particularly in N scale. The NMRA has settled on a standard DCC socket for HO and these make installation easy. Some engines in both N and HO are offered with decoders already installed.

• Intimidation. Because DCC systems are so sophisticated and can do so much, they sometimes frighten modelers away. Those throttles with dozens of buttons can look scary, as do the thick manuals full of unfamiliar words.

• Unfamiliarity. Reliable command control has been around for almost 20 years, DCC has been out there for three, but still most modelers have never had the opportunity to visit a layout equipped with command control and see the difference it makes in running trains.

Why DCC?

Before the DCC standard was established all command control systems were proprietary. One company's command station would run only that company's receivers (the pre-DCC word usually used for decoders).

Compatibility has been achieved with DCC, but it's important to understand just how far that goes. The standard applies only to the decoders. That translates to all the decoders in your engines not having to be the same brand. Also, you can take your engines over to a friend's house and run them on a system different from yours. Leave your throttle at home, though, as it probably won't work.

If you're interested in DCC and learning which system might be good for you, you'll need to do some research. I've listed manufacturers and you can call them or write for information. Most are MR advertisers, so consult the Index of Advertisers. If you have a friend (preferably smart) who has a system and is happy with it, consider getting the same for yourself so you'll have someone to call on when you can't decipher the manual. If your hobby shop is a dealer for a particular brand, consider choosing that one strongly.

Learning to use a DCC system is quite similar to learning to use a computer. In the beginning it can be quite frustrating, but with time it gets much easier. Once you get started in command control, whether with a DCC or a proprietary system, you'll probably learn to love it. It's a great way to run a railroad. ✿

Fig.1 CONVENTIONAL TRAIN CONTROL

Only 1 engine or set of engines can be controlled in a single electrical block

Track power

Power pack

Fig. 2 TYPICAL DCC CONTROL

Messages to decoders

Engines are under independent control in a single electrical block

Track power

Power booster

Command station

Throttles

Illustration by Phil Kirchmeier

Manufacturers of DCC systems

CVP Products
P. O. Box 835772-M
Richardson, TX 75083
http://www.cvpusa.com

Digitrax
P. O. Box 1424
Norcross, GA 30091
770-441-7992
http://www.digitrax.com/

Lenz Agency of North America
P. O. Box 143
Chelmsford, MA 01824
508-250-1494
http://www.lenz.com/

LGB of America
6444 Nancy Ridge Dr.
San Diego, CA 92121
619-535-9387
http://www.lgb.com/

Model Rectifier Corp.
P. O. Box 6312
Edison, NJ 08818-6312
908-225-2100
http://www.btown.com/mrc.html

North Coast Engineering
1900 Empire Blvd.,
Suite 303
Webster, NY 14580
716-671-0370
http://www.ttttrains.com/northcoast

Ramfixx Technologies
P. O. Box 341
Lewiston, NY 14092
905-542-2347
http://ourworld.compuserve.com/homepages/ramtraxx/

Wangrow Electronics
1500 W. Laverne, Box 98
Park Ridge IL 60068
847-696-3294
http://www.wangrow.com/

Railroading without derailments

Easy ways to keep 'em on the track

BY JIM HEDIGER

During my Ohio Southern RR open houses I've often overheard comments like:

"I'll never be able to get my trains to run this well."

"Wow! Did you see how they could back those long coal trains?"

Comments like these certainly boost one's ego, but any modeler can achieve the same results. It's just a matter of understanding the critical relationships between track, wheels, and couplers. Here's what I've learned in 30 years of building and operating HO scale layouts.

Track

Good track is at the top of the list. Some modelers prefer handlaid track, but I've had excellent results using commercial track and turnouts. The brand isn't important, but the way you install the track affects its operating qualities. On the Ohio Southern, I freely intermix brands and rail sizes.

The key is to maintain good alignment through the rail joints. You need a smooth path for the wheels to follow so make sure the tops and inside faces of the railheads match perfectly. Any misaligned rail ends, kinks, or rough edges are potential derailment sites.

Normal rail joints connecting pieces of the same size rail are the easiest to make. See fig. 1. Make sure your rail joiners fit snugly, the rail ends are cut squarely, and both rails are straight through the joint. Lean down and squint along the rail to check and adjust the alignment. You also may need to trim a little off the tie tops to eliminate any hump at the joiner.

For joints between different rail sizes, I begin by adding thin styrene shims under the ties to gradually raise the lighter weight track until it matches the heavier. You want the tops of the rails aligned across the joint as shown in fig. 2. Next I add metal shims inside the joiner to support the smaller rail. Carefully align the rail ends so their tops and inside faces match perfectly, and then solder the joint.

I finish up by gently smoothing the top and inside face of each joint with a jewelers file. Slide a fingernail across the joint and use a flat file to remove any rough spots you can feel. Once your fingernail slides smoothly over the joint, the wheels will also pass without difficulty.

Turnout tuneup

A little tuneup is all it takes to get reliable operation from most commercial turnouts. Start by obtaining the National Model Railroad Association standards gauge for your scale. Use it to check the gauge through the turnout.

Most commercial turnouts have switch points with blunt ends as shown in fig. 3. Use a jewelers flat file to bevel the inside of each point to a knife edge. This provides a smoother transition for the wheels to follow as they roll from the stock rail onto the switch point. Here again, I use the fingernail test to check and eliminate any rough spots.

I've found many commercial turnouts are a bit tight in gauge at the points. Use the NMRA gauge to check the spacing between each switch point and its opposite stock rail. I've found that some switch points are thicker than others so a turnout may be in gauge on one route but not the other. Correct any tightness by filing the point thinner.

Look closely at the frog – it should also have a sharp point. If it doesn't, use the jeweler's file again to sharpen it. The NMRA gauge has pins to check the spacing of the long guardrails that protect the frog. These guardrails should engage the back of the outer wheel's flange to guide the wheelset away from the frog point. If the guardrail

Darla Evans

Use a National Model Railroad Association standards gauge to check the spacing of each wheelset. Correct or replace any wheelset that doesn't match the notches in the gauge.

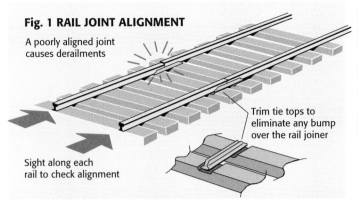

Fig. 1 RAIL JOINT ALIGNMENT

A poorly aligned joint causes derailments

Sight along each rail to check alignment

Trim tie tops to eliminate any bump over the rail joiner

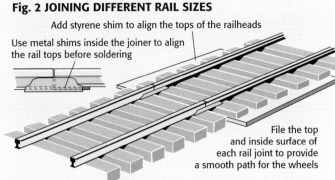

Fig. 2 JOINING DIFFERENT RAIL SIZES

Add styrene shim to align the tops of the railheads

Use metal shims inside the joiner to align the rail tops before soldering

File the top and inside surface of each rail joint to provide a smooth path for the wheels

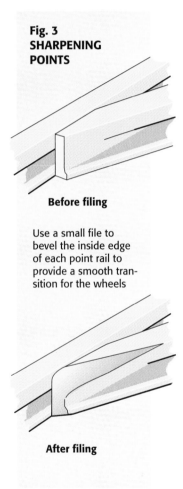

Fig. 3 SHARPENING POINTS

Before filing

Use a small file to bevel the inside edge of each point rail to provide a smooth transition for the wheels

After filing

spacing isn't correct, the inner flange will hit the frog point as shown in fig. 4.

You can correct plastic flangeways that are too wide by adding a shim cut from .010" to .020" brass sheet to the guardrail so it will pull the wheelset clear of the frog point. Cement the shim in position with cyanoacrylate adhesive (CA). After the cement sets, file the shim smooth and use a metal blackener to conceal it.

Trucks and wheels

Trucks are included in most car kits, but you'll find there's a wide range of quality. The typical rigid acetal plastic truck frames are usually good, but the wheelsets are marginal.

Kit wheelsets are seldom all in gauge, so you'll need to check each one with the NMRA gauge. If respacing is needed, grip the axle with a pair of pliers and use your fingers to twist the wheels along the axle. Recheck the wheel spacing and make sure they're centered on the axle.

Roll the wheelset down a slight incline to see if the wheels are concentric and mounted squarely. If a wheel wobbles from side to side or has an off-center axle, discard it.

I learned a long time ago that good wheelsets are probably the best single investment you can make to improve train performance. This discovery came after I noticed that hopper cars seemed to be involved in most of my derailments. Since they're the most heavily used car type on my layout, I decided to replace the wheelsets on any hopper that derailed.

The sudden improvement in operating quality was immediately noticed by my operators and this convinced me to continue. Within a few months all of the hoppers had new wheels and their operating performance was nearly

perfect. As a result, I continued the replacement program until every car on the OS rides on precision wheelsets made by Jay-Bee, Kadee, or NorthWest Short Line.

Whenever I replace wheels, I make sure the new wheelsets turn freely in the sideframes. Then I mount one truck with its kingpin screw tightened down until the truck rotates freely without rocking from side to side. The second truck is left looser so it can rock beneath the carbody. This creates an effective three-point suspension that allows the car to pass over uneven spots or turn-outs with ease.

Couplers

Knuckle couplers are the most popular among experienced modelers. Kadee is the recognized leader here, offering an extensive line of couplers with different shanks and mounting hardware to fit nearly every locomotive and car on the market.

Intermountain Ry. Co. and R. C. Henry Co. (McHenry brand) both offer new acetal plastic knuckle couplers that are compatible with the Kadee Magne-Matic couplers. I reviewed them in Product Reviews in the February 1996 MR.

All of these automatic couplers work well, but take care to follow each manufacturer's installation instructions to obtain the best results. Every coupler should move freely and center properly. Make any vertical adjustments required so all couplers match the recommended height on the NMRA gauge. Be especially careful to adjust the trip pins for proper clearance above the rails. This is a close tolerance that spells disaster if the pin is too low.

Motive power

The Ohio Southern operates with a good-size fleet of readily available plastic diesels. Athearn, Atlas, Kato, Proto 2000, Proto Power West, and Stewart models predominate. I check every locomotive's wheels with an NMRA gauge and make adjustments or replacements as needed.

No mystery

When you get right down to it, there really isn't any mystery to building a smooth-running railroad. Most of what I do falls into the tune-up category and just taking the time to do things right the first time. That may take a bit longer, but it certainly pays off as visitors watch a trio of my SD40s backing a unit coal train smoothly into the power plant. ✿

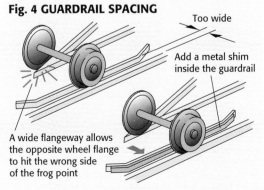

Fig. 4 GUARDRAIL SPACING

Too wide

Add a metal shim inside the guardrail

A wide flangeway allows the opposite wheel flange to hit the wrong side of the frog point

Illustrations by Robert Wegner

This Centerline Products track cleaning car cleans lots of rail quickly, and comes in all the popular scales.

Cleaning track and wheels

Secrets of trouble-free operation

BY ANDY SPERANDEO
PHOTOS BY REBECCA SALITURE

Clean track and wheels are about as basic to model railroading as you can get. Our electrically powered trains depend on good electrical contact between wheels and rail. This is just as true of today's high-tech command control systems as it's always been for the simplest train-set power pack, and in every scale from the smallest to the largest.

We have several good ways to keep track and wheels clean today, and these are some that work for me.

Abrasives

The old standby for cleaning track is a rubber block with abrasive particles that you rub along the rail like an eraser. The best-known of these is the Bright Boy, sold by Wm. K. Walthers as catalog no. 949-521. It's inexpensive and easy to use, and is especially good for very dirty track.

When you've been painting or ballasting track or building scenery, an abrasive cleaner may be the only way to get trains running again. In those cases it's also a good idea to clean the inside corner of each rail, where wheels with rounded contours make most of their contact.

Another trick of the trade is the "Bright Boy on a stick," a cleaning block mounted in a homemade handle, for reaching into through truss bridges, tunnel portals, and other places where hands and arms may not fit.

But beware: Abrasive cleaners leave minute scratches on the rails, and these can give dirt places to hang on and build up. They also leave rubber and abrasive granules behind. Many model railroaders prefer to use abrasive track cleaners only when they're really needed and use gentler cleaning methods most of the time.

Track cleaning cars

There are two track cleaning cars that I find most effective. The first is simply an ordinary "house" car – boxcar, stock, or refrigerator car – with a Masonite pad riding rough-side down and sliding along the track. I first saw such "slider cars" on the legendary HO scale Gorre & Daphetid RR of famed hobbyist John Allen. He had several of these cars in his roster and simply operated them in regular trains to keep the rails polished. Before each operating session, we operators cleaned the pads with sandpaper, and the black streaks of dirt on the pads before sanding showed that the sliders worked.

It's easy to make your own slider cars, but A-Line, a division of Proto Power West, offers kits for what it calls "track shiner pads." The HO kit is no. 10003 and no. 10004 is for N scale. A-Line's kits include retainers to hold the pads in the cars when you pick them up, but I wouldn't use them because it's easier to clean the pads when you can just drop them out of the car.

The other track cleaning car I recommend is the roller type made by Centerline Products in N, HO, S, O, and G scales. These use a heavy roller wrapped with heavy-duty paper towel material. The roller turns as the car is pushed or pulled along, and again, black streaks on the toweling show that this car is effective.

This car can also be used with liquid cleaners, and the manufacturer recommends Goo Gone, a citrus-based solvent available in supermarkets. We've used this combination with excellent results on our Kalmbach employees' club layout, the Milwaukee, Racine & Troy. I follow Centerline's suggestion and wrap a thin strip of masking tape around the toweling, so we can push or pull the car without unwrapping the towel.

Liquid cleaners

Besides Goo Gone, electronic contact cleaners can make good liquid track cleaners. Model railroaders have used one called No-Ox for many years. A favorite of long-time MODEL RAIL-ROADER editor Linn Westcott, No-Ox is available from Craftsman Specialty Supply, 6567 Forty Mile Point, Rogers City, MI 49779, a mail-order source for modeling supplies and tools. Another similar cleaner is GC Electronics Contact Kleen, sold by electrical and electronics suppliers.

With these you apply the cleaner sparingly to the rails for two or three feet and run an engine over that section of track. The wheels spread the cleaner around the layout. They're especially useful when you have contact problems during an operating session and don't want to stop what you're doing to clean track.

Cleaning wheels

Locomotive pickup wheels need to be just as clean as the track. Most model diesels made today pick up from all wheels, and that makes it easy to clean them. Spread a paper towel across the track and dribble a little Goo Gone where the towel rests on the rails. Then hold your diesel in place with one truck on the towel and the other truck directly on the rails, and apply power to spin the wheels. When you see those satisfying black streaks on the towel, you can turn the diesel around to clean the other truck.

For other locomotives, especially traditionally wired steam engines, the Kadee no. 236 Speedi Driver Cleaner does the trick. It has alligator clips to attach to rails or a power pack and brass-bristle brushes to clean the wheels. It works on engines from HOn3 through O scale.

Finally, don't forget the wheels of your cars. They may not pick up current, but when dirt is allowed to build up on wheel treads it can cause wobbly running and even derailments if it's deep enough to "hide" the flanges. The solution here is really simple: the same paper towel across the track with Goo Gone applied along the rails. Roll the car back and forth by hand a few times and its wheels will be clean. You'll find model railroading is a lot more fun with clean wheels rolling on clean track. ☼

The Bright Boy abrasive track cleaner is an old standby that's still very useful. It can be mounted in a homemade handle to clean those hard-to-reach places.

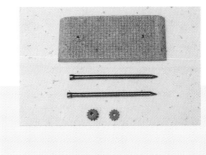

A-Line's kits convert any 40-foot HO or N scale house car into a track cleaner.

SLIDER TRACK CLEANING CAR

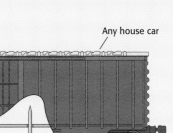

Any house car

Masonite cleaner pad, slightly wider than track, edges beveled, rough side down

Nails glued to pad fit loosely into holes drilled in car floor, so pad can follow irregularities in track

Illustration by Rick Johnson

With liquid electrical contact cleaners like No-Ox, a little goes a long way.

A paper towel, some Goo Gone, and a length of track will let you clean the wheels of both locomotives and cars.

Diesel locomotive tune-up

Easy tricks to improve performance

BY JIM HEDIGER
PHOTOS BY THE AUTHOR

The first trip of a new locomotive is something model railroaders look forward to with great anticipation. Our imaginations run wild with visions of a prototype's smooth start as the new model leans into the couplers and begins to pull. From this point on, smooth performance is essential to the imagery.

Most of the current diesels are sold "ready to run," but a little tuneup can make a big difference in any locomotive's performance. Older models, like any mechanical devices, will also benefit from an occasional tune-up.

The model shown here is an Athearn GP60 which has one of the hobby's most popular mechanisms. Athearn's mechanism is simple and reliable and it set the pattern for most of today's HO scale models, even though competitors may vary the snap-locks and the shape of some components.

Inspection

The first step is to remove the body. Most diesel mechanisms have cast lugs which fit into openings on either side of the body shell to hold the two together. If the sides are spread slightly, the chassis will drop free. Recent Athearn models have clips which pass through slots in the bottom of the fuel tank. Grip the fuel tank in one hand and gently rock the body slightly from side to side to release the chassis as shown in fig. 1.

Set the mechanism on the track and observe how it operates. A stuttering motion is symptomatic of electrical problems caused by dirty wheels, corroded contacts, or frayed wiring. If there's a recurring slow speed hesitation, look for binding in the mechanical parts. If a truck doesn't sit level, some parts may not be fully seated.

Wheel cleaning

Poor electrical contact affects performance more than any other single factor and dirt is usually the culprit. Attach test leads to the motor connections and hold the frame upside down in your hand. Turn on the power so the engine runs and then use an abrasive block to polish the wheel treads to a nice shiny surface.

Note: Never use steel wool for any of this cleaning. Small shards of metal break off and are attracted to the motor where thay may cause a short circuit or other damage.

Mechanical checks

Any slow speed hesitation requires disassembly of the trucks to check the gears. Work on a clean bench and take one truck apart at a time to keep from losing anything or mixing up the parts. Use a small screwdriver to gently pry off the retainer that holds the worm assembly on top of the truck as shown in fig. 2. Take note of how the universal joints fit together as you remove the truck.

With the truck off, polish the electrical contact surfaces around the kingpin on both the truck and the underframe. See fig. 3.

Spin the wheels in the truck with your finger. If the gears turn smoothly there's no reason to open the gearbox. If you detect a bind, pop off the retaining clip and carefully open the gearbox. See fig. 4. Inspect the gear edges and hubs for molding flash (excess plastic), chips, or dirt. Lay the gears down in order on the bench and check the inside of the gearbox castings. Remove any stray material and then use detergent and warm water to wash all the parts.

While the truck is apart, check the wheel spacing with a National Model Railroad Association standards gauge as shown in fig. 5. Make any needed adjustments by gripping both wheels in your fingers and twisting them in or out of the molded gear. Don't forget to check the axle gears for flash or dirt.

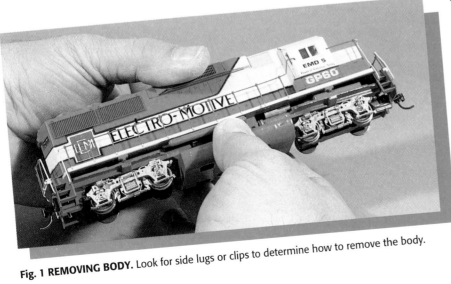

Fig. 1 REMOVING BODY. Look for side lugs or clips to determine how to remove the body.

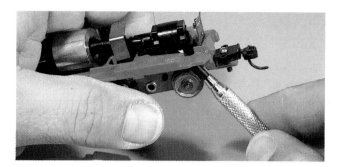

Fig. 2 REMOVING WORM HOUSING. Use a small screwdriver to gently pry off the combination worm housing and truck retainer.

Fig. 3 TRUCK KINGPIN. Polish all electrical contact points where current is transferred between mechanical components.

Lubrication

Very small amounts of lubrication will do the job on model locomotives. A single small drop of plastic-compatible light oil will suffice on the bearings (I use Labelle no. 108). Don't add any further oil unless something squeaks. During my years as a hobby shop repairman, I saw more problems from too much oil than anything else.

Reassemble the truck and add a drop or two of model grease to lubricate the gears. See fig. 6. Each gear's teeth should be covered with a thin film of grease, but you don't want it to spread. Labelle no. 102 grease is my choice as it's formulated for use on plastics. Make sure you use the right type as some lubricants attack plastic or may cause parts to swell or become brittle.

Fig. 4 GEARBOX. Clean off any molding flash or dirt found in the gearbox.

Electrical pickup

A good electrical path from the rails to the motor is essential. Begin by cleaning and checking every contact point where current is transferred between components.

Some models have tiny phosphor bronze fingers which rub against the wheels to pickup current. Remove any lint that's trapped in these pickups and adjust their tension for good contact.

Finally, look for any frayed wiring or loose connections. Replace any defective wiring with flexible wire, but be careful soldering so you don't damage any nearby plastic parts.

Athearn models come with a steel contact strap that I replace with flexible wire, as shown in fig. 7, to improve the electrical path. To do this, remove the steel strap and cut off the truck extensions about ¼" beyond the motor clips. Solder a piece of flexible wire to the top center of the strap and add a short piece of wire to one end for the headlight connection. Snap the shortened strap on top of the motor, bend the wires around to reach the trucks, and then solder one end to each truck bracket. Finally, shorten the headlight contact and solder the short wire to it.

Final inspection

Reassemble the chassis, test run it, and then wash your hands so you don't fingerprint the body with lubricants that may affect the paint job. This is a good time to check and repair any body damage, replace missing details, touch-up nicked paint, and adjust couplers.

It takes only a few minutes to tune up a locomotive, but it makes a world of difference in realistic performance. After you try it, I'm sure you'll agree it's time well spent. ☸

Fig. 5 GAUGING WHEELS. Use an NMRA standards gauge to check the spacing of all the wheelsets and correct any problems.

Fig. 6 LUBRICATION. Apply only a couple of drops of plastic-compatible lubrication in each truck gearbox.

Fig. 7 NEW WIRING. Replace the original Athearn steel contact strap with flexible wires soldered in place to provide a more reliable electrical path.

Kadee HO couplers

An introduction to Magne-Matic automatic knuckle couplers

BY JIM HEDIGER
PHOTOS
BY THE AUTHOR

Many modelers don't care for the looks of the horn-hook couplers supplied with most HO train sets and plastic car kits. Kadee couplers are more realistic in appearance and perform better. These automatic knuckle couplers are sold under the Magne-Matic trademark in many variations for easy installation on all sorts of rolling stock.

Magne-Matic couplers resemble the prototype knuckle couplers, although they're nearly 50 percent larger. A tiny lip inside the knuckle prevents uncoupling as long as there's tension pulling across the couplers.

Magne-Matic uncoupling takes place only over a magnet, and only when slack releases the knuckle lips.

A useful feature of Magne-Matic couplers is delayed uncoupling. If the cars are separated and then brought back together over a special wide magnet, both couplers shift off-center to the "delayed" position shown in fig. 1. You can then gently shove the delayed car to any location beyond the magnet as long as the push is smooth and steady.

Couplers

Kadee's no. 5 couplers, shown in fig. 2, are the most popular. They include a stamped sheet-metal spring that drops right into the coupler boxes molded on most plastic car kits. See fig. 3. Or you can mount them in the plastic box Kadee includes in case there's no box or the stock box won't work.

Most Kadee couplers are zinc-alloy castings, but some are molded in plastic for use where metal couplers may cause a short circuit.

Several different shank lengths are available including some with the coupler head offset up or down. These can be used in unusual mounting situations. Some of these coupler sets include special coupler boxes and springs to replace the original manufacturer's parts.

If you send a large, self-addressed envelope, stamped with 52 cents postage, with your request, Kadee will be happy to send an information packet with all the coupler dimensions. The firm's address is 673 Avenue C, White City, OR 97503-1078. Kadee also sells a no. 13 sample kit that includes all 25 different couplers and a pair of uncoupling magnets.

Installation

Kadee supplies excellent illustrated instructions with each package of couplers. Take the time to read them as they contain useful tricks for top performance.

Some kit coupler boxes are wide enough to let the no. 5 centering spring rotate so it won't center the coupler properly. Adding some thin styrene shims along both sides of the box will take care of this problem.

Sometimes it's easier to remove the entire original coupler box and replace it with the Kadee box. In such cases, assemble the coupler in the box and secure the lid with just a touch of liquid plastic cement. Mark and drill a no. 50 hole on the car's center line, then attach the box to the floor with a no. 2 round-head screw.

Coupler height

Correct height is critical to the operation of Magne-Matic couplers. Kadee's no. 205 coupler height gauge makes it easy to check this dimension. Just set the car and gauge on the rails as shown in fig. 4. The "air hose" may need to be bent a little until it lightly touches the gauge's bottom platform. If the knuckles line up you're all set, but misalignment indicates some adjustments need to be made.

Most cars are low, so add washers to the truck kingpins to raise the carbody. Kadee sells no. 208 red washers (.015" thick) and 209 gray washers (.010" thick) for this purpose.

It the model is high, you'll need to look at the clearance between the wheels and the car-body. You can trim either the truck or body bolsters to lower the body as long as the wheels don't touch the floor. An alternative is to use Kadee no. 211 shims between the floor and the coupler box.

Using more than a couple washers or shims may affect the car's overall appearance. If so, it's time to check into the other styles of Magne-Matic couplers. You'll find there's probably another draft-gear box or an offset coupler that'll fit perfectly and still preserve the model's looks.

Uncouplers

Kadee makes four uncouplers:

• No. 307 is an electromagnet intended for high-traffic areas. It's activated by remote control only when it's needed. A hole must be cut through the roadbed and track board to mount this magnet beneath the track.

• No. 308 is a large permanent magnet to be concealed under the track. The magnet is 1/4" thick and is easy to install in a recess cut or routed into the roadbed and trackboard.

The no. 308 magnet has another drawback. Its magnetic field is strong enough to attract steel axles which may create enough momentary slack to cause an unwanted uncoupling. To avoid this, Kadee and others sell replacement wheel-sets with non-magnetic axles.

• No. 312 is a narrow permanent magnet that mounts between the rails for uncoupling only (it isn't wide enough to operate the Magne-Matic coupler's delay feature).

• No. 321 is a wide permanent magnet that mounts between the rails on top of the ties. It's wide enough to activate the delay feature.

Truck-mounted couplers

Many HO train sets come with horn-hook couplers mounted on car and locomotive trucks. This arrangement works fine with short freight trains; however, backup moves are a problem as the couplers tend to skew the trucks sideways and cause derailments. Kadee makes couplers for train set cars and they help reduce this skewing problem as the pressure is straight through the Magne-Matic couplers instead of sideways.

Most modelers prefer body-mounted couplers so switching impacts and train pressures are passed through the carbodies. This reduces truck skewing and lets backup moves track better through switches and curves.

Decision time

If you're new in the hobby and Magne-Matic couplers appeal to you, the time to change is now. It's much easier to convert your present equipment right away and then apply Kadee couplers to your future purchases than to make a massive conversion after you've built up a large roster. ⚙

Fig. 1 DELAYED COUPLERS. Bringing Magne-Matic couplers together over an uncoupler shifts them off center so a car may be pushed and left at any spot beyond the magnet.

Fig. 2 NO. 5 COUPLERS. This typical package of Kadee couplers includes centering springs, coupler boxes, and couplers for two cars.

Fig. 3 COUPLER BOX. Kadee's no. 5 coupler drops right into the coupler boxes found in most plastic car kits.

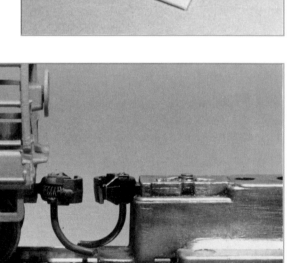

Fig. 4 COUPLER HEIGHT. Correct height is critical to smooth operation, so Kadee sells this coupler height gauge that makes it easy to check each installation.

Micro-Trains N scale couplers

How to convert to good-looking, good-operating couplers

BY KEITH THOMPSON

Do you want reliable operation, a more realistic look, derailment-free uncoupling, and remote uncoupling from your N scale couplers? Then take a look at Micro-Trains couplers. Most seasoned model railroaders prefer them to the Rapido-type. Just push two cars together and they couple. That's not really a big deal, the Rapido-style couplers that come on many N scale cars and locomotives do the same thing. The big difference comes in the uncoupling.

Micro-Trains couplers rely on magnetism for uncoupling, so there's no contact between the coupler and the uncoupling ramp to derail equipment. As shown in fig. 1, Micro-Trains couplers also feature a delayed uncoupling action that lets you uncouple over the ramp and push the car or string of cars to where you want without recoupling.

Micro-Trains uncoupling ramps are a little different from normal magnets since they're polarized along their narrow axis (normal bar magnets are polarized on their wider axis). This means you'll have to use Micro-Trains uncoupling ramps to automatically uncouple cars and locomotives.

Uncoupling magnets

If you want to use Micro-Trains' automatic uncoupling feature, then you'll need to consider uncoupling magnet styles and locations. Micro-Trains makes two types of uncoupling magnets; between the rails, and beneath the track. See fig. 2. Each style has its advantages and disadvantages.

The between-the-rails magnet is the easiest to install but the least esthetically pleasing. It can be disguised as a road crossing and that's about it. You can buy it installed in a 5" straight section of Atlas track as Micro-Trains no. 1311 or by itself as no. 1310. The no. 308 is a permanent under-the-tie uncoupler that can be hidden under ballast but has to be recessed into the roadbed before laying the track.

One alternative to the ramps is to "pick" the couplers apart with a small tool. Place the flat tip of the tool between the couplers, twirl gently, and they'll uncouple. Rix Products no. 24 is a plastic tool that does this type of uncoupling the best.

What couplers to use

Micro-Trains offers several dozen coupler styles for just about any locomotive or car. They all couple with each other but they feature different shanks for a variety of mounting situations. Micro-Trains sells a manual called the *N-Scale Coupler Conversion Guide* that covers installing and adjusting couplers for almost any piece of N scale equipment. See fig. 3.

Another item Micro-Trains offers to help you pick the right coupler is the no. 1050 N-scale coupler starter kit. It includes samples of several

SP 496532

Micro-Trains couplers not only look more realistic, they greatly enhance N scale operation. Besides selling couplers and trucks for converting other makes, Micro-Trains sells its own line of N scale freight cars, like the ACF covered hopper here, that come equipped with its couplers.

style couplers that come on some N scale equipment. Here's basic information about them and their operation:

Micro-Trains or Kadee?

If you're new to N scale you've probably heard experienced modelers talking about Kadee N scale couplers and cars. These are the same as Micro-Trains. A few years back Kadee was divided into two independent companies, with Kadee making HO scale and larger products and Micro-Trains carrying forward with N scale and Z scale.

How they work

Micro-Trains couplers are spring-loaded so they can automatically couple like the proto-

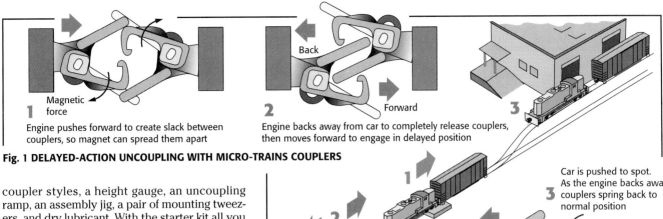

1 Magnetic force
Engine pushes forward to create slack between couplers, so magnet can spread them apart

2 Back / Forward
Engine backs away from car to completely release couplers, then moves forward to engage in delayed position

Fig. 1 DELAYED-ACTION UNCOUPLING WITH MICRO-TRAINS COUPLERS

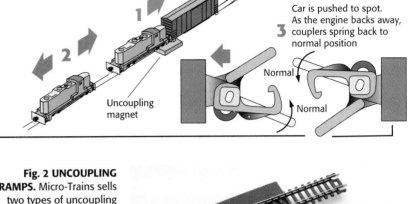

3 Car is pushed to spot. As the engine backs away, couplers spring back to normal position
Normal / Normal
Uncoupling magnet

coupler styles, a height gauge, an uncoupling ramp, an assembly jig, a pair of mounting tweezers, and dry lubricant. With the starter kit all you need to decide on is if you prefer truck-mounted or body-mounted couplers.

Truck or body mounted?

In other scales truck-mounted couplers are a no-no, especially in switching where they cause derailments while being pushed. In N scale they work just fine thanks to the deeper wheel flanges and proportionately larger-radius curves. They work so well, in fact, that Micro-Trains uses truck-mounted couplers on its own line of N scale cars.

Going the truck-mounted coupler route is the easiest way to convert cars that come with Rapido-style couplers. Micro-Trains makes truck and coupler assemblies, so all you do is take the stock trucks off and put the Micro-Trains trucks on.

You may hear that there's a movement underfoot in N scale to body-mount Micro-Trains couplers on cars for esthetic reasons, but for most modelers the truck-mounted couplers work fine. For locomotives, however, body-mounting is the best because the front end of the engine is always visible and the large pilot openings or separate pilots that allow truck-mounted couplers to swing are unrealistic. Micro-Trains makes conversion kits for some diesel models that fill the opening and body-mount the coupler in one step.

Once your couplers are mounted, use the no. 1055 gauge to check the coupler height. See fig. 4. Use the thin metal gauge that comes with the no. 1055 to check the height of the trip pin. If the pin is too high the couplers won't uncouple reliably over uncoupling ramps, too low and it might snag on turnouts and crossings. If you're using the truck-mounted couplers you rarely have to adjust anything.

Finding more information

Your local hobby shop can show you the complete line of Micro-Trains couplers and help you decide which ones to use for your equipment. The *Micro-Trains Conversion Guide* is a must-purchase item as well as the no. 1050 starter kit. However, after you've been using them awhile the installation will be almost second nature.

Try Micro-Trains couplers for your N scale equipment and you'll see how much of an improvement they are. The good looks and better performance are worth the expense of converting your equipment. ⚙

Fig. 2 UNCOUPLING RAMPS. Micro-Trains sells two types of uncoupling ramps. The no. 1311 above-the-ties uncoupler on the right is easier to mount but the no. 308 below-the-ties uncoupler looks better after the track is ballasted.

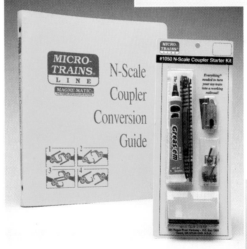

Fig. 3 BEGINNERS AIDS. Micro-Trains N-scale coupler starter kit no. 1050 includes everything you need to test installations and install couplers. The conversion guide shows what Micro-Trains couplers work best on what equipment.

Fig. 4 ADJUSTING THE TRIP PIN. After your Micro-Trains couplers are mounted you'll need to make sure their height is correct using the Micro-Trains no. 1055 height gauge. The correct height for the trip pin is .010" above the railhead.

Hardshell scenery

A simple shell turns benchwork into realistic landscape

BY JEFF WILSON

The biggest transformation a model railroad undergoes is when bare benchwork is covered with a scenic shell. Hardshell scenery, using plaster (or similar material) in a self-supporting scenic form, has been a popular method of creating scenery since the 1960s when it was popularized by long-time MODEL RAILROADER editor Linn Westcott. It's still among the easiest ways of building good-looking scenery.

Scenery intimidates many modelers, especially beginners. This needn't be the case. Building scenery can be somewhat messy, but it's actually quite easy. More importantly, it's very forgiving – if you make a mistake or if an area doesn't turn out as you wanted, just cut out the offending section and start over.

As you plan scenery, remember to keep the ground rolling. In real life the ground is almost never completely flat, even in the plains areas.

Supporting the hardshell

Webs of corrugated cardboard strips offer good support for hardshell construction, as shown in fig. 1 and the color photograph. This method is inexpensive and easy. You can use the track subroadbed, backdrop, and layout front edge for supports. Brace large hills in the middle using scrap lumber.

Hot glue works well for holding the cardboard web together. Hot glue sets fast, so you can create large forms quickly. Staples are good too, and you can purchase a heavy-duty

Jim Forbes

You can see how the various scenic layers work over this open-grid benchwork. The cardboard web supports a shell of plaster-impregnated gauze wrap. A layer of Sculptamold over this serves as the scenic base. A coat of tan paint and some ground foam, and the scenery is complete.

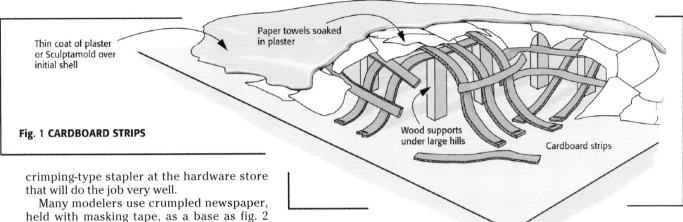

Thin coat of plaster or Sculptamold over initial shell

Paper towels soaked in plaster

Fig. 1 CARDBOARD STRIPS

Wood supports under large hills

Cardboard strips

crimping-type stapler at the hardware store that will do the job very well.

Many modelers use crumpled newspaper, held with masking tape, as a base as fig. 2 shows. This can be more difficult to control, as the wads of paper tend to go where they want to. Misting the paper with water helps control this. The lumpy texture of the newspapers works well for creating rugged scenery, such as mountain foothills.

Ideally, it's good to remove the paper wads once the hardshell is dry. The shell will support itself, and many modelers don't like the idea of having a pile of tinder-dry newsprint lurking under their layouts.

The basic shell

Plaster has been the hardshell material of choice for many years because it's inexpensive and easy to find. Many modelers prefer Hydrocal, a brand-name plaster that sets up very hard. Other varieties, including common plaster of paris, will work just fine.

To form the shell, mix a small batch of plaster to pancake-batter consistency. Dip pieces of paper towel into the plaster, then apply them to the supporting base. Thick towels, such as tri-fold towels made for commercial towel dispensers, work well.

The main disadvantage of this method is that it's messy. Be sure to cover your track, and use newspapers or a drop cloth to protect the floor.

Another material that's become very popular is plaster-impregnated gauze, as shown in the photograph. Woodland Scenics Plaster Cloth and Activa Rigid Wrap are two brands. To use it, simply cut the material into small pieces, dip a piece in water, and add it to the base. It's not as messy – there's no mixing or dripping plaster to contend with. A disadvantage is the cost, which could make it prohibitive for large layouts.

Adding a final coat of plaster over the shell adds strength and provides a smooth surface for ground cover. Wet the shell with a spray bottle of water, then spread on a thin coat of plaster. Smooth the plaster with a wide (2- to 4-inch) wet brush.

Another material that works well is Sculptamold, a plaster-like material made of pressed paper fibers. Sculptamold is another material that's nearly mess-free. It's easy to work with, but it's more expensive than plaster. Smooth it with a small putty knife, spoon, or wet brush.

Many companies make cast-plaster rocks, as well as latex-rubber molds so modelers can

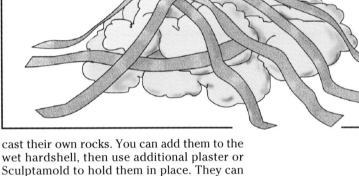

Fig. 2 WADDED NEWSPAPER

Masking tape

Newspaper

cast their own rocks. You can add them to the wet hardshell, then use additional plaster or Sculptamold to hold them in place. They can be painted and stained using a combination of artist's acrylic colors and ink. See the article on the Soo Line's Red Wing Division in the December 1994 MR for examples.

Ground cover

Paint the shell with earth-color latex paint, then sprinkle ground foam in place. Woodland Scenics and AMSI make a wide variety of colors and textures. Fix the ground cover by spraying it with diluted matte medium or white glue (about 1 part medium or glue to 3 parts water) with a few drops of dish detergent added. Matte medium is an acrylic varnish you can buy at art supply stores. It dries clear. The dish detergent will help the diluted matte medium soak into the scenery material.

Having a green cover over everything takes your layout a giant step up from bare benchwork. You can then add trees, shrubs, and other scenic details as you wish. We'll cover some of these topics in future Basic Model Railroading columns.

That's all there is to it. When you're ready to build scenery, I strongly recommend getting a copy of Dave Frary's book, *How to Build Realistic Model Railroad Scenery* (Kalmbach). The book goes into great detail on various techniques, and shows how to add water, trees, roads, rockwork, and many other scenic details that make a layout come alive. ✿

Scenery colors and textures

BY JIM KELLY
PHOTOS BY
DARLA EVANS

There are lots of good ways to shape model railroad scenery, and Jeff Wilson covered several popular methods in his April 1995 Basic Model Railroading article on hardshell scenery. Here we're assuming that you have, by hook or by crook, arrived at a terrain surface that you now wish to color and detail.

Again, there are lots of ways to do it, but I want to present a "water-soluble" system of compatible materials as popularized by Dave Frary in his book *How to Build Realistic Model Railroad Scenery* (Kalmbach Publishing Co.). Dave's book is the best reference available, and I recommend you invest in a copy.

Why water-soluble materials?

Water-soluble materials are, quite simply, paints and other products that can be mixed with water. Acrylic paints fall into this category, and run the gamut from house paint to artists' colors in tubes. Such water-based materials offer some big advantages:

• They are much safer than solvent-based paints, with no fire hazard and no dangerous chemicals nor noxious fumes.

• The only thinner you need is as close as the nearest water faucet. Cleaning brushes and other equipment is easy too, using water and a little detergent.

Painting rocks

On a model railroad you'll find two basic types of scenery surfaces to finish, bare surfaces (rocks for example), and surfaces to be covered with earth, grass, or vegetation.

Let's start with rock surfaces. In nature rocks can be just about any color imaginable. For modeling a specific area your best bet is to work from reference photos. If your rocks are generic, then shades of gray and brown usually work best.

If you feel unsure about painting rocks (most of us do the first time), why not start by building a simple cliff you can paint at the workbench? You can paint it one way, let it dry, then paint it white and try again.

Figure 1 shows a basic rock painter's kit. For generic rocks you'll need a selection of earth colors, so called because historically they were pigments made using minerals from the earth itself. Raw umber, burnt umber, raw sienna, and burnt sienna will get you going. You'll also need titanium white and mars black. All these are available in tubes in art supply stores. Good brands are Liquitex and Grumbacher. You'll need some inexpensive brushes; they need not be high-quality. Three flat brushes in 2", 1", and ½" widths will get you started and you can develop your own preferences later.

Let's paint

Some modelers prefer to paint colors directly onto raw plaster, but I do better if I paint the rocks white first. To paint with tube acrylics, first squeeze a bead of paint, say 1" long, onto a palette, a plate, or some other mixing surface.

Dip your brush into clean water, then dip the tip into your bead of white paint and start

Drybrushing highlights
the detail on model rocks.

brushing it onto the rocks. You'll soon get the hang of adjusting the thickness of your paint.

Next squeeze out beads of the colors you want to use. Dip your brush into water, into the white, then into the colors you want to combine. Mix them a bit and start brushing them on. You'll get more realistic results if you don't mix the paints too thoroughly, work quickly, and keep changing the mix as you go. Also change the water frequently.

I like to work fast and get a basic coat of paint over the entire area, then go back in and begin reworking one place and then another. You can create all sorts of interesting effects by working one color in on top of another.

You'll also find that a household spray bottle filled with water can be one of your handiest painting tools. You can spray water on the paint to get it to flow into hard-to-reach places. Spray hard and you can wash off effects you don't like.

Let the paint dry thoroughly and then redo any areas you don't care for. Let them dry thoroughly again and then you can brush on a thin wash of black or other dark colors to settle in the cracks and crevices and create three-dimensional effects. Let this dry thoroughly and then you're ready for the finishing touch, drybrushed highlights.

Dip the tip of a 1/2" brush in paint straight from the tube and wipe it on a paper towel until nearly all the paint is gone. Then stroke lightly downward on the your rock surfaces. The idea is to highlight details with just traces of paint, making them look as if they were being struck by sunlight. Use your basic colors lightened considerably with white, and also use some white itself straight out of the tube.

The most important thing is, as the Nike commercials say, to just do it. Before long you'll discover nuances in technique that work for you.

Modeling ground cover

The first step many modelers take in modeling the ground is painting it with a flat tan latex paint. Avoid dark colors or your layout will look really somber. The paint can be inexpensive house or wall paint. If you should buy high-quality paint you'll probably want to thin it about half with water to get the best results, otherwise it'll tend to fill in the detail. We use the paint not only as a coloring agent, but also as an adhesive for scenery materials.

Liberally paint the area of ground you want to work on, then begin sprinkling on a variety of scenery materials. You can sprinkle on some real dirt or sand to represent bare places.

A popular product for representing grass and foliage is ground foam, which is simply foam rubber dyed various colors and ground to various grades. One brand found in most hobby shops is Woodland Scenics.

You can make some nifty foam dispensers by punching holes in the tops of recycled small glass jars, although I've always managed well just sprinkling the material on from paper or plastic cups.

Variety is the key. You want some brown to show through here and there, and you don't

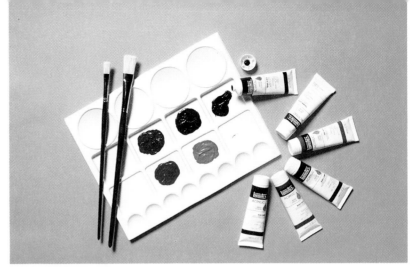

Fig. 1 BASIC ROCK-PAINTING KIT. Here's all you need to become an expert rock painter. With a little practice you'll soon be surprising yourself.

Fig. 2 COVERING THE GROUND. More is usually better when it comes to adding ground foam to a scene. You can always soak the material with diluted matte medium and sprinkle on more layers.

want all the foliage to be the same color or have the same texture.

Even though we're using the paint as an adhesive, it will secure only a thin layer of material. We get the most realistic results with ground foam when we build it up in layers, using a variety of colors and textures.

To make these materials adhere, spray them with adhesive as you go along. One popular bonding agent is matte medium, a clear, flat acrylic sold in art supply stores. See fig. 2. You can mix one part of this with six parts water, add a few drops of dishwashing detergent to help it penetrate the scenery materials, and apply it with an inexpensive household spray bottle, the type sold for misting plants and found in supermarkets and hardware stores. Wet the scenery materials thoroughly.

Once the adhesive dries the scenery will be firmly bonded but appear to be lying loose and natural. You can keep spraying and building up materials for as long as you care to.

We have so many good scenery products to work with today that anyone can make a good-looking model railroad. Give it a try and you may be surprised to discover that a talented artist is lurking inside you. ⚙

Using rock molds

The MR&T gets a quarry

**BY GEORGE
SEBASTIAN-COLEMAN**
PHOTOS BY THE AUTHOR

Winter Hill on MODEL RAILROADER's own club layout, the Milwaukee, Racine, & Troy, is supposed to be home to a rock quarry. During the initial push to get the benchwork covered with scenery, however, all it got was a steep grassy slope. Now the time had come to turn that grass slope into a rock wall.

There are many ways such a wall could be constructed, but the most popular method is casting plaster in latex rock molds.

Making your own

It's fairly easy to make your own rock molds. The hardest part may be locating a rock, or rocks, with enough surface detail to be interesting at a scale size; coal also works very well.

Once found, clean the rock surface of dirt and paint on a layer of liquid latex, let dry, and repeat. After you've made several layers, it's a good idea to place a layer of gauze over the mold and attach it with another layer of latex. One or two more latex layers will result in a mold that will withstand many castings.

For those who don't care to make their own, many excellent rock molds are sold in hobby shops.

Choosing the molds

Rocks come in many varieties and the mold you choose, whether commercial or homemade, should represent an appropriate type for your area or scene. I wanted clearly stratified rock to represent lannon stone, a common building stone quarried in nearby Lannon, Wis.

You can use the same mold several times by turning the casting upside down, breaking it in pieces, or just putting it next to different castings. For a quarry, even greater repetition is okay because the mechanical process of removing the stone creates a more regular surface than found in nature.

Plaster

Though Hydrocal is often recommended, U. S. Gypsum no. 1 casting plaster or plaster of paris is perfectly satisfactory and costs much less. If you're doing a large layout, it's worth your time to find a source for large quantities of plaster, typically 50- or 100-pound bags. Check the Yellow Pages under plaster.

Always mix plaster by adding plaster to the water. The ratio should be about two parts plaster to one part water by volume. This produces a pancake-batter consistency. Water-based paints or dry pigments can be added to the water to give a base color to the casting.

Spray the mold with water mixed with a drop of detergent. This will help the plaster fill the mold and act as a release agent after it has set.

Pour the plaster into the molds, poking it into crevices with a finger or stick, and let it begin to set. Molds with a lot of relief may require support to hold them level. Wadded newspaper or almost any scrap material will usually suffice.

If you want to place the mold on the scene while still wet, you need to time it so the plaster is no longer runny but has not yet begun to crystallize. Before placing the mold, lightly wet your base plaster so that it doesn't suck the water from the casting.

Winter Hill Quarry was made using only three molds, but it'd be hard to find the repetitions.

The Superior Products and Woodland Scenics molds are typical commercial products. Scene Tints are water-based paints that can be used before casting.

After making several castings from each of the molds, I began stacking them against the slope to see how they fit together. Don't forget to try turning them upside down or breaking them into smaller pieces to get more variety.

Placing molds and filling gaps

Once the plaster has set, peel off the mold and examine your casting. A few small bubbles are nothing to worry about. You can ignore them, fill them, or try scraping across them to blend them with the casting. If you have a large cavity, you need to be more careful when you pour. Don't throw away the casting though. You can break it and use pieces, or even fill the hole.

You can set castings in place with plaster, white glue, or hot glue – hot glue sets quickly so is handy on steep slopes. Once your castings are in place, fill the gaps between them with more wet plaster using sticks, putty knives, brushes, fingers, anything that will get it where you want it. Before it sets hard, carve the fill material to blend with the castings

Don't worry if some filler drips across your casting – you can readily chip it away with a putty knife. Use the putty knife or other tools to blend the joints and the castings.

These two molds were applied to the slope while the plaster was still wet. The molds weren't removed until the plaster had thoroughly set.

Painting and finishing

I used artist's acrylics to paint my finished wall. In addition to black, white, and the standard earth tones of burnt umber, raw umber, burnt sienna, and raw sienna, I used a yellow and a deep purple. The yellow was to give the proper color to my Lannon stone, and purple is yellow's complement so it grays the yellow.

I brushed a yellow wash over the whole surface, followed by a thin wash of brown mixed from my earth tones. Thin washes of darker browns were added in a few places, especially under outcroppings. Next, I drybrushed some white in horizontal streaks to highlight a few areas. Finally, India ink diluted in alcohol was sprayed over the whole surface to deepen the crevices and tone down the whole effect.

Some of the castings were broken apart and rearranged. Whole castings and pieces were attached to the hill with hot glue.

The last step is to blend the rocks into the surrounding scenery. Sift dirt and loose rock (broken up pieces of castings make a fine talus slope) around the castings. A few bits of foliage, even trees, are usually found in natural crevices. Since this is an old wall of the quarry, a few plants have even sprung up on my wall.

For more ideas for rocks and finishing the scenery, I recommend Dave Frary's *How to Build Realistic Model Railroad Scenery*, available from Kalmbach Publishing Co. and hobby shops. ✿

This rock outcropping was made using a pocket mold – a very deep mold that needs to be supported when the plaster is poured.

Three kinds of trees in various sizes and shapes spruce up this HO scene. Note how the taller trees are used in the foreground while smaller ones add depth.

How to make realistic trees

Basic techniques for sprucing up your foliage

BY MELANIE GOHDE AND GEORGE SEBASTIAN-COLEMAN
PHOTOS BY WILLIAM ZUBACK

Trees – everyone wants them on their layout, but no one wants to take the time and effort needed to make them. Whether you need to forest a hillside or just add a few well-placed foreground trees, here are some tips for making quick, realistic trees using commercial products. On the opposite page, we take you step-by-step through constructing two kinds of deciduous trees and one conifer.

Here are the tools and products Melanie and George used to make the trees shown in this article. On the left is a side cutter, used for trimming thicker limbs and wire trunks. On the right is a sprue cutter for smaller branches.

But first, some basics. Go outside and look at some trees. Unlike the ones you drew as a child, real tree trunks aren't brown but grayish, the leaves aren't all exactly the same shade, and treetops aren't perfectly round. Heights, shapes, and types vary widely.

When you add trees to your layout, variety is the key. Use several different kinds, but choose species based on the geographical area you model. Planting an odd number of trees in each grouping usually looks best.

One caveat before we begin: Many trees on layouts are too small. Unless they're very young saplings, trees should be taller than trains. So use shorter trees like the 3"-5" ones from Woodland Scenics described on the next page in the background, and make taller trees for the foreground. As an example, the sycamore trees in the above photo are a scale 60 to 65 feet tall, a realistic height for that kind of tree. Now let the tree making begin! ⏣

FOREGROUND DECIDUOUS

1. This is processed and colored plant material from the Forest in a Flash kit we used (Jane's Trains, 8221 Ferguson Rd., Dallas, TX 75228). Accurate Dimensionals offers a similar kit.
2. Pluck the leaves with tweezers (don't forget the small ones at the branch joints). Paint all the branches: We used Polly Scale Reefer Gray. As shown in the round photo, hold the branch upside down and work the paint into the joints.

3. Gather branches until you're happy with the shape of the tree. Wrap thread around the trunk then secure with cyanoacrylate adhesive (CA). Attach smaller branches with CA.
4. To thicken the trunk, dip into Mod Podge (or any acrylic gel medium). For a thicker trunk, substitute acrylic latex caulk, applying with a toothpick from the bottom up. Finally, paint the trunk the same shade as the branches.

BACKGROUND DECIDUOUS

1. To make a Woodland Scenics Realistic Tree, remove the base with a sprue cutter. Keep it to use while drybrushing.
2. Drybrush the trunk gray (see round photo): Put some paint on a paintbrush, brush the excess onto a paper towel, and apply light strokes to eliminate the plastic shine while bringing out trunk details. Next twist the branches, shaping each major limb before concentrating on the individual branches.

3. Apply Woodland Scenics Hob-e-Tac (or a liquid contact cement like Goo) to the ends of branches, then dip the tree into the kit's foliage bag (break up the chunks into smaller pieces). After it's dry, remove excess foliage – less is more.
4. In a well-ventilated area, spray the foliage with an adhesive or hair spray then sprinkle on a lighter shade of Woodland Scenics Blended Turf to add color variation and texture.

CONIFERS

1. This is a Faller blue spruce tree right out of the package.
2. Here we've given one tree a haircut. Use a side cutter or scissors to trim away branches to form a trunk and to thin out and vary the shape of the tree. Dip the trunk into Mod Podge and let dry. We painted the trunk Reefer Gray then drybrushed on Accu-Flex Green Drab (any dark brown or brownish-green will work) to bring out the bark's texture.

3. Use the larger trees in the foreground and the smaller ones in the background or in new-growth areas. We've sprayed this tree with an adhesive and sprinkled on some Woodland Scenics Blended Turf (see round photo).
4. Adding various shades of Blended Turf allows you to change the color of the tree and adds texture making it suitable for foreground use.

Let's model water

The secret's in the shine

BY JIM KELLY

As with most other things in model railroading, there is no single best way to model water. The method I'll show you here is easy and works every time, but there are lots of other effective ways. For more information on modeling water, as well as on every other phase of building scenery, let me recommend Dave Frary's *How to Build Realistic Model Railroad Scenery*, available from our publisher, Kalmbach Publishing Co., and sold in hobby shops.

To sum up the method shown here, I paint the water black, let the black dry thoroughly, then paint on a coat of gloss medium, a shiny clear acrylic paint sold in art stores.

"Now hold on a minute," you might say, "Why'd you paint the water black? Everybody knows water's blue, not black."

To which I'd answer, "I painted the water black because it works," which is a pretty good reason for doing anything. Also, water isn't really blue, but colorless. Much of the time water looks blue to us because it's reflecting a blue sky. On cloudy days the water looks gray. The color we see when we look at a body of water is in fact reflected.

Fig. 1 JOINT COMPOUND. To eliminate the plywood texture Jim applied a thin layer of joint compound.

The technique I'll describe here works because the surface acts like a mirror. Nearly all the light that penetrates to the black is absorbed, so that what you mostly see is the light bouncing off the shiny surface. So much for physics – let's model.

Making waves

What sort of surface you start with doesn't matter, as long as it's level. It's no secret that water tends to lie flat. Here we're starting with plywood, so we need to get rid of the surface texture. Whatever else we might say about water's characteristics, it doesn't have wood grain.

As shown in fig. 1, I coated the plywood with joint compound, applying it thinly with a putty knife. If you want to model a quiet pond you need go no further, but I wanted small waves on my river so I let the joint compound set for a few minutes and then dabbed it lightly with a dampened household sponge. See fig. 2.

The thicker the joint compound the higher your waves will be, so it's important to keep it thin. Keep in mind that in HO scale a scale foot-high wave measures about ⅛". In N scale that same wave would be a two-footer, so if you're not careful your waves can start looking like crashing surf.

The joint compound will need a day to dry and, providing you didn't put it on too thick, will not crack. If it does, the stuff is water soluble, so you can brush out the crack with a wet paintbrush.

To illustrate this story Jim Kelly added a riverbank to Marty McGuirk's N scale diorama.

Fig. 2 MAKING WAVES. Dabbing lightly with a household sponge added some wavy texture.

Fig. 3 BLACK PAINT. Inexpensive black latex paint was brushed on next.

Color and shine

Next, as shown in fig. 3, I painted the joint compound black, using plain, ordinary latex paint. It doesn't matter if it's flat or gloss because the shine is added in a separate step.

Now what's needed is a gentle transition from the shore line to the water, otherwise your bank will look like the edge of a well. This I accomplished with a ½" flat brush and some of the same tan latex paint I'd used to paint the scenery. See fig. 4.

Dip the brush slightly into the paint, then start at the water's edge and work out. As the paint in the brush is used up you'll be able to "feather" the tan color out into the black. If you decide you've gone too far in a place or two, let the paint dry throughly, then drybrush your way back in with black.

The final step is brushing on gloss medium. See fig. 5. One word of warning: Stir this finish carefully, but don't shake the bottle. Shaking leads to air bubbles, and you want a nice smooth finish.

That's it. You've got a nice looking body of water, and don't be surprised if you have to wipe the finger prints off occasionally. Some of your visitors won't be able to resist touching it to check if it's really wet. ✿

Fig. 4 BANK DETAILING. Feathering the tan earth color out into the black made for a natural-looking transition.

Fig. 5 THE FINAL TOUCH. Gloss medium adds shine to the water. Polyterrain is a brand found in hobby shops.

Building believable bridges

BY KEITH THOMPSON

How to add a solidly supported span to your railroad's right-of-way

Often when building our lay-outs we leave a span of plywood where a bridge should be because we're not all that sure about the kind of bridge that belongs there, how to build it, or how to blend it into the layout. Luckily, it's easier than you think to replace that improbable plank with a believable bridge.

Bridge basics

Figure 1 shows four commonly used bridge types. It's possible for all of them to be used together for one span, but it's rare to see more than two types of bridges used together. Railroads tend to keep their bridges as simple as possible because the more types of bridges, the more complicated the piers get.

What's under the bridge has a lot to do with the type that's selected. A bridge crossing a wide, fast-moving stream will usually be a truss type with concrete or stone piers. Wooden tres-tles are used for crossing flood plains and for approaches to steel spans. Simple deck girders are preferred where the span is short and the bridge won't cause clearance problems under-neath. Through girders are used where clear-ances are a problem.

The best way to figure out which bridge to use is to look at the prototype and use your noodle. You can also consult reference books on the subject like Kalmbach's *Model Railroad Bridges and Trestles*. It's available through your local hobby dealer.

Figure 2 shows the main parts of a through plate-girder bridge and its support structure. Abutments and piers are similar for all bridge types. Notice the step in the abutment for the pedestals: to be realistic a model abutment must have this step.

Bridge decks and track

There are two types of bridge decks, open and ballasted. Any steel or wood bridge can have an open deck, one where you can look between the ties and see the bridge's structure. Track used on open-deck bridges is different than regular railroad track. The ties are usually thicker and always more closely spaced. Open-deck bridges are popular with real railroads because they're cheaper to construct. Modelers like them also for their visual interest.

Ballasted-deck bridges use regular track sup-ported on ballast sitting in a concrete, steel, or wood trough. Prototype ballasted-deck bridges are usually through girder bridges and concrete trestles. Model railroaders like them because they don't need special bridge track and are easier to build.

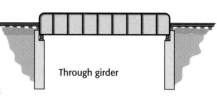

Through girder

Fig. 1 COMMON TYPES OF BRIDGES

Bridge track may also include guardrails. These help keep derailed cars from damaging the bridge structure. Guardrails usually begin well past the ends of the bridge so they can guide errant wheels back in line with the rails before the car or locomotive reaches the bridge.

Building bridges

Unless you're modeling a specific prototype, the best way to build a bridge is to start with a kit. At least one of each type is made in HO and N scales. The toughest part will be choosing a kit that suits your skill level, time constraints, and budget.

Most bridge kits are plastic, but some are wooden craftsman kits. There are also plastic kits like the ones made by Bridge Master and Central Valley that fall into the craftsman cate-gory. It's a good idea to save those until you have a couple of simple plastic bridge kits under your belt. After you know how bridges go together, craftsman kits are fun to build and very rewarding.

To model open-deck bridge track, you have several choices. In HO scale Walthers and Micro Engineering both sell bridge track with code 83 rail. The 19^{11}/$_{16}$"-long Walthers track comes complete with guardrails but the 7"-long Micro Engineering track only has the close tie spac-ing. You'll have to use transition joiners if the rest of your layout uses a different size rail.

For N scale, Micro Engineering makes 36"-long code 70 and code 55 bridge track with sep-arate guardrails that you can add when and where they're needed.

Planting your bridge

Now that you have a bridge ready to go, you need to plant it firmly in your layout's scenery so it looks like it belongs. Figure 3 shows the method that works best for me.

First, remove the temporary span and test-fit the bridge, abutments, and piers to check clear-ances. If you're using a commercial bridge abut-ment or pier, there's a good chance you'll need to shorten it to fit.

If your track's not already attached to the bridge go ahead and fasten it. Since commercial

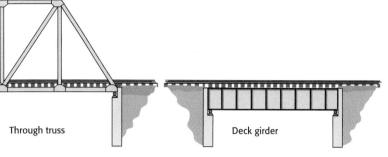

Through truss

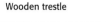
Wooden trestle

Deck girder

bridge track is made of slippery engineering plastic, use a sticky adhesive like Walthers Goo to hold it to the bridge. Longer bridges will also need checking with a straight edge to keep everything in line and avoid sagging. Use twist ties to hold the bridge to the track until it dries.

Add cleats to the subroadbed and attach the abutments to them with Liquid Nails or hot glue, making sure they firmly touch the bridge's bottom or pedestals. You want it to look like the abutments are really supporting the bridge. Do the same with any piers.

Now "backfill" around the abutments and piers with scenery. Because it's more controllable in tight spaces, I like to use a fiber-filled plaster product called Sculptamold. It's made by American Art Clay Co., and is available at most hobby dealers.

Begin by building up the areas behind the abutments. You want them to look like they're really holding back the dirt. Next, bring the ground below the abutments and piers up over their bottoms. They need to look firmly planted.

Add the final scenery material over the area you just finished and then bring the ballast up to the bridge. On open-deck bridges, there always are special ties or boards sitting on each abutment to keep the ballast from falling over the edge. These are often called dump boards. If you don't have them yet, make some out of plastic or wood and add them now so you can ballast up to them.

There you go, your bridge is in and ready for the next train, and it sure looks a lot better than a piece of plywood! ◘

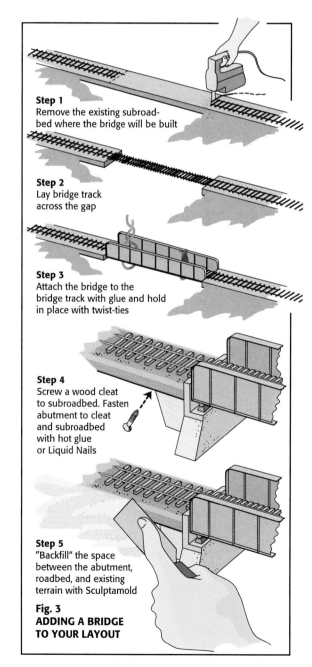

Step 1
Remove the existing subroadbed where the bridge will be built

Step 2
Lay bridge track across the gap

Step 3
Attach the bridge to the bridge track with glue and hold in place with twist-ties

Step 4
Screw a wood cleat to subroadbed. Fasten abutment to cleat and subroadbed with hot glue or Liquid Nails

Step 5
"Backfill" the space between the abutment, roadbed, and existing terrain with Sculptamold

Fig. 3
ADDING A BRIDGE TO YOUR LAYOUT

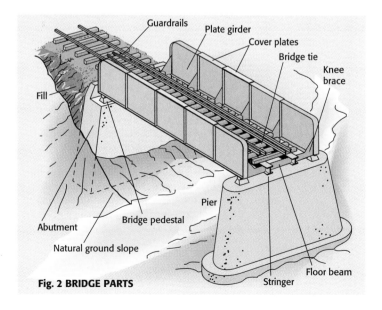

Guardrails
Plate girder
Cover plates
Bridge tie
Knee brace
Fill
Abutment
Natural ground slope
Bridge pedestal
Pier
Floor beam
Stringer

Fig. 2 BRIDGE PARTS

Plastic kit basics

Some terminology and tips for working with plastic kits

Apply liquid cement from the inside to avoid marring the plastic surfaces.

**BY GEORGE
SEBASTIAN-COLEMAN**
PHOTOS BY JEFF WILSON

Jeff, Marty, and I, all colleagues here at the magazine, were talking about our early model building attempts. Remembering our own confusion over what a pin vise was or how every plastic airplane we ever built was made with parts twisted off the sprues, we thought that perhaps others out there could use some basic terminology and tips about plastic kits.

To build any kit you'll need some tools. Figure 1 shows the basic tools I recommend for working with plastics and includes a brief explanation of what they do.

Injection molding

Most of the kits you're likely to buy, whether of structures or rolling stock, are made of "injection-molded plastic." That means molten plastic is forced into an enclosed mold which is a negative image of the part or parts to be made. The plastic travels to the parts along tubes called "sprues." Where a sprue connects to a part it usually tapers down to a small point.

Most parts are made in simple two-part molds. Where the two halves meet is called the "parting line." If plastic has seeped between the halves of the mold this creates "flash," a thin sheet of plastic. "Ejector pins" are used to push, usually from the backside, a finished casting out of the mold. They often leave a circular indentation and sometimes a ring of flash.

The word sprue also is used to refer to a group of parts all connected to one main, tree-like sprue. Figure 2 shows parts being trimmed from a typical multipart sprue.

Kit inspection

Before doing anything else you need to inspect your kit. Instructions for kits range from little more than an exploded-view diagram (all the parts are shown with arrows indicating how they connect together) to very detailed step-by-step manuals. You may find that some craftsman kits are actually easier to build than some beginner kits just because their instructions are so much clearer.

All instructions should include a "parts list." Don't do a thing until you've matched each part with its name or number. Some kits have drawings showing the parts still on the sprues with "callouts" (a label with a line pointing to the part) identifying each piece. These illustrations are a big help when there are a lot of parts.

Once you know all the parts are there and which is which, read the instructions – all of them. If all you have is an exploded view, take the time to figure out in what order you'll assemble the parts, and write it down.

Basic preparation

It's best to remove from the sprue only the parts you're going to need in the next step. That way they're less likely to get lost. Even if you plan to paint some parts before assembly, it's usually easier to paint them on the sprue and retouch any areas you file or sand later.

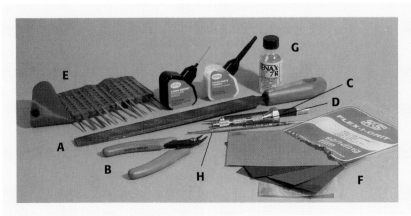

Fig. 1 BASIC TOOL KIT. A. 8-inch mill file for cleaning up sprue marks and parting lines. Buy a new one. **B.** Sprue cutters are flush-cutting pliers sold by many manufacturers. Don't use them for anything else. **C.** Hobby knives for clean up and removing parts. **D.** Needle files for removing flash, parting lines, and sprue marks. **E.** A pin vise holds small drills for hand drilling. If you're adding detail parts or changing coupler types you'll want one. **F.** Fine sandpaper, 440 grit and higher. **G.** Liquid styrene cement produces clean joints and sets quickly. Also pictured is Testor's clear cement for glazing windows. **H.** Fine brush for applying liquid cement.

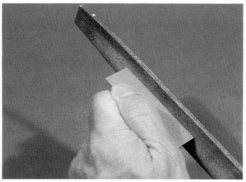

Fig. 2 REMOVING PARTS. Put the flush side of the cutter against the part and squeeze gently. Be sure and cut each sprue feeding the part.

Fig. 3 MILL FILE. A large file keeps edges straight for strong glue joints and good looks.

Check each part for parting lines and flash. Especially on small parts it may be easier to clean up the part before removing it from the sprue. Remove parts with your sprue cutters as shown in fig. 2. Sometimes there isn't enough room to get the cutters between a part and the sprue. In this case support the part on a cutting surface and slice through the sprue with a hobby knife.

Now clean up any remaining sprue material or parting lines. For straight edges, use the large mill file first, as in fig. 3. This assures that the edges stay straight. To clean parting lines or flash in windows or along uneven edges, use a hobby knife, needle files, sandpaper, or any combination of them, as shown in fig. 4. Always use the largest file possible to avoid creating uneven edges.

Especially on cylinders, like tank car bodies and water tanks, you may find parting lines or joints between parts in the middle of large smooth surfaces. Use needle files to remove the line or smooth the joint, then polish the surface with sandpaper. Start with nothing coarser than 600 grit and keep getting finer – Flex-I-Grit by K&S is available in a combination package of very fine grits, the finest of which will put the polish back on the plastic.

Assembly

Probably the single most important tip here is to keep things square. The first step is to have a good, flat work surface. Self-healing cut-ting mats (the nicks from your knife disappear) are available at any fabric store and many hobby shops.

A "square table" has fences on two sides to keep parts at right angles. You can build your own by gluing a couple of pieces of 1 x 1 to a piece of plywood. Just use a square to make sure they're at right angles. Commercial tables are also available; the one in fig. 5 is made of steel and has magnets to hold parts in position while you glue them.

The second big tip is to use the minimum amount of glue necessary. Where possible, mate the parts to be joined and apply glue from the inside with a small brush.

Plastic cement is a solvent; it actually softens the plastic. If you get some on the surface of your model, let it dry and then start polishing the blemish with sandpaper as described for parting lines. Excess glue can also cause the plastic to warp.

The final step on most structures is "glazing" the windows; that is, installing whatever material is being used to represent glass. This should be done after you do any painting, so figure out how you're going to reach the windows before you begin. Sometimes it's easiest to paint and glaze the window frames separately, then add them to the building at the end.

I hope the terminology here will help you follow some of our other articles, and I'm sure if you follow these basic tips you'll find your kit-built structures look neater and more realistic. ⊘

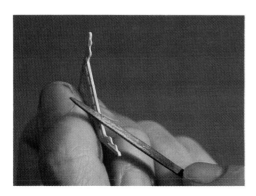

Fig. 4 NEEDLE FILES. Cleaning off the parting line makes this wood timber look more realistic.

Fig. 5 SQUARE TABLE. A square table keeps corners square until the cement dries. Micro-Mark sells a similar unit as a "magnetic gluing jig."

Individualizing kit structures

Minor alterations, paint, and signs not only make
a building your own, they make it right for your layout

**BY GEORGE
SEBASTIAN-COLEMAN**

With the hundreds of easy-to-build plastic structure kits on the market, it may seem you wouldn't have to worry about your buildings looking like everyone else's. Yet many of these kits have been around longer than most of us have been in the hobby, and their looks are as familiar as old television stars.

More importantly, your layout may need a hardware store, but the kit that caught your eye, and that fits the space on your layout, is called a mattress factory. Don't let that stop you! A little rearrangement of the parts and the application of some readily available decals can make that off-the-shelf kit into the perfect industry for your pike.

I'm not talking "kitbashing" here (combining pieces of several kits into a new building), just little things to make the kit your own. Nor is this a step-by-step article. I just want to give you some ideas you can apply to any of the kits on the market.

Choosing the kit

My main reasons for choosing Model Power's two-story Western Union office (no. 452) are ones you should consider.

Many plastic kits combine the same basic structure with different details to create new kits. When choosing one for your layout, look at all the variations and pick the one that seems closest to what you want or which simply has the most parts – whatever pieces you don't use will probably be useful elsewhere.

This kit included lots of extra details, and it could be used for many eras.

Deciding what changes you want

Before starting, take time to look over the plans and imagine how you could make simple changes, or just repaint your kit to create your own version. Also look through the decals at your hobby shop or in catalogs for ideas.

I was able to build the balconies as a separate unit and move them around the building. Even if I hadn't been able to do that, I'd still have held the parts next to one another to get a sense of what fit where and how it would look.

Other readily changed features of this kit are the rooftop water tank and shed, and the attached garage. Each of these is a complete structure in itself and so can be placed anywhere, or modified as I'll describe later.

After looking over the kit and the signs on two sets of Microscale decals (industrial signs no. 87273 and city signs no. 87275), I decided to do two versions – a restaurant with apartments above it and a small machine shop. The first step for both versions was moving the building into the twentieth century.

Ken's Bar and Grill

Few modern commercial buildings have balconies on their front walls. However, balconies are still common on the backs and sides of buildings, serving as fire escapes and "backyards" for many apartment dwellers. Just by moving

Ken's Bar and Grill has rooms for rent upstairs. Paint plus relocating the balconies gave this kit a whole new look.

Darla Evans

50

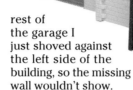

Built per the instructions, the boardwalk, balcony, big signboards, and saloon-style doors give the Western Union office an Old West appearance. The modern garage door, however, works against this look.

Jim Forbes

the balcony to the back, I changed the Old West building into a twentieth-century structure.

The only other changes I decided to make were to leave off the rooftop shed and the garage, though the garage could be placed next to the building or across an alley.

The one problem with modernizing this kit is the front door. Those saloon doors would look out of place on most any building except a saloon. I decided to just glue a piece of Evergreen scribed styrene behind them. After painting, I used a pencil to darken the center scribe line to indicate the two doors. You could also substitute doors from other kits or from detail suppliers like Grandt Line Products.

I assembled the basic building including the windows and my door addition, but I didn't glue in the roof or attach the water tank and shed. Then I built the balconies as separate units and painted everything. Normally I wouldn't add the windows until after I painted the walls, but it wasn't much trouble to paint them in place.

Leaving off the balcony until later is almost a necessity to have room to do the painting. If I couldn't assemble something like this separately, I'd still wait until after painting the walls and then assemble it in place.

I used Modelflex Gloss Red darkened with a few drops of their Gloss Green for my brick color. After this was dry, I painted the mortar lines by slopping thinned Accuflex Sand over the whole surface and wiping it off with a damp paper towel. Then I painted the windows and doors Modelflex Antique White. I used Reefer Gray for the water tank and balcony assembly.

Because this is a combination restaurant and apartment building, I kept the rooftop water tank. I decided to leave off the shed though, as it seemed to clutter up the roof line.

The last touch was applying the Microscale decals for Ken's Bar and Grill, the vacancy sign to suggest the apartments upstairs, and a 7-UP sign and thermometer to the front door.

Superior Gear Co.

I imagined this change as if it had happened to Ken's Bar and Grill, so you can still see the faded part of the old sign above the doorway. This was done by sanding the old decal with very fine sandpaper.

This time I solved the front-door dilemma by replacing the kit's front-window and door unit with the whole front wall from the garage. The

rest of the garage I just shoved against the left side of the building, so the missing wall wouldn't show.

I pulled the water tank off and put the shed back on the roof. My thinking was that a machine shop didn't need the reserve supply of water pressure, but it did need a hoist, and the mechanism for this is in the shed. I also left off the balconies because they were unneeded either as porches or fire escapes – though a fire marshal might disagree with me.

I'm pleased with how my buildings turned out, and I know that no one else has any just like them. If you take a little time to imagineer your own version before putting your next kit together, I'm sure you'll be equally pleased with your own individualized structure. ⚙

Jim Forbes

While trying to decide what color to paint the roll-up door, I took a second look at the decals for the Superior Gear Co. – and painted not only the door but the brick filler and all the other windows with Modelflex C&O Yellow to match the signs.

Carefully placed road signs, a billboard, crossing gates, figures, and vehicles draw viewers into the N scale Carolina Central and help direct their attention to specific areas. One story told by this picture: New road signs were just put up marking the curve at the bottom of the rocks. These were added after a car missed the turn. Skid marks (made with black chalk) on the road are still a vivid reminder of the accident.

Add life to your layout with details

Well-placed signs, vehicles, and figures help draw attention to scenes

BY MELANIE GOHDE
PHOTOS BY REBECCA SALITURE

When we last visited the N scale Carolina Central (January 1997 MODEL RAILROADER), associate editor Marty McGuirk mentioned several possibilities for detailing the layout. Using figures, vehicles, detail parts, signs, and some styrene for scratchbuilding, I developed several detailed scenes that enliven this layout while directing the viewer's eye.

Getting started

How do you know where – and where not – to add details? The first rule is don't go overboard. Ensure that everything you add to your model railroad makes sense. You don't need to detail every scene or put up every possible sign; leave neutral, less "busy" areas between detailed scenes. If you couldn't explain how or why something got where it is, leave it off.

Figure out where you want your visitors to look, then add something to capture their attention. Trying to keep them away from the unfinished edge of the layout? Bring them into the middle with interesting scenes.

Remember that in most cases people observing your layout are looking down on it – like the view from a helicopter – so things such as rooftops will be readily visible and are a natural area to detail. I included access hatches and vents on the tops of the buildings downtown.

Adding realistic elements

Here's the approach I took: I looked around the Carolina Central, noting scenes that had potential and brainstorming for what could go into those areas. Using the theme of the layout (a rural Southern town), I came up with several storylines and scenarios that I could develop.

Next I thumbed through Walthers' N scale catalog, jotting down items I could use and ideas.

These are some of the detail parts used for this story. With a coat of paint, a little weathering, and an imagination, they can help add life to a layout.

The downtown square is a busy place: elderly ladies read the plaque on a war hero's statue, a couple realizes the restaurant is closed, and a worker takes out the trash.

There are many detailing possibilities for a house: wash hung out to dry, a sign in the front yard, a mailbox, trash cans, a gravel path, and neighbors talking. Last-minute repairs are being made on the car that's for sale – it still needs a lot of work!

Realizing that I didn't have the space or time to develop all of those concepts, I concentrated my efforts along the road that runs through town, focusing on the mill, a house, and downtown.

Once I had all the parts, vehicles, and signs I wanted to use, I painted the details and arranged them on the layout. After relocating the pieces several times, I finally glued everything down with cyanoacrylate adhesive (CA) and weathered the items with pastel chalks to blend them into the scenes.

Look at the photos to see what I did specifically, but remember, those are just ideas. The parts listed below give you a starting point – use your own imagination based on your layout.

Finishing touches?

You'll never be "done" detailing. You'll constantly see more possibilities or a manufacturer will offer something you must have. Perhaps you want to remove some details in an overly done area, or you're adding a new building and want to draw attention to it. Bear in mind that you need to have both attention-getting and neutral areas, or you'll have overkill as scenes run into one another, creating a cluttered look.

So take a trip to the hobby shop or grab a catalog to get ideas. The potential is endless. Just remember: Be creative, use your imagination to develop stories related to your layout's theme, but don't overdo it – in this case, less is more. ⚙

Bill of materials

Accu-Flex paint
16-05 Weathered Black
16-11 Concrete Gray
16-32 Santa Fe Silver
16-85 Reading Green
16-98 Camouflage Brown
16-99 Flat Dull Gray
16-101 Medium Field Green
16-103 Armor Sand

Bachmann
42520 assorted autos

Blair Line Signs
P. O. Box 2291
Lee's Summit, MO 64063-7291
005 traffic signs
007 traffic signs
010 traffic signs

051 Main Street storefront signs
052 safety and miscellaneous signs
055 signs for industries
066 billboards with posts

Cal Freight
12652 Pleasant Place
Garden Grove, CA 92641
1000 roof access stair cover
1010 large boxes, pallet stack
1050 wood crate, medium short
1095 freight sacks, pallet stack
1100 freight sacks, piles/stacks
1120 tree stumps, small
1150 dumpster, open loaded
1165 roof access hatch
2015 cyclone roof vents, small
2020 cyclone roof vents, large
2075 cabinets

Evergreen styrene
220 .035" rod
9040 .040" sheet
153 .060"-square strip
234 .438" tubing

GHQ
51004 Ford F-150 pickup truck

Kato
23500 assembled plastic autos

Miscellaneous
Pastel chalks

Preiser figures
79019 standing pedestrians
79036 truckers
79095 shopping promenade
79099 male commuters
79102 workers

Add life to your layout with figures

Simple techniques for painting scale people

BY JEFF WILSON
PHOTOS BY THE AUTHOR

Few things give life to a scene like scale figures. Seeing miniature people in and around buildings, sidewalks, parks, and streets makes cities and towns appear lived-in and active.

Several companies make nicely detailed scale figures. Preiser makes a wide variety of injection-molded plastic figures in scales from Z to G. Other companies offer plastic and cast-metal figures in sets or individually.

One problem of factory-painted figures is the finish. All too often figures are painted in an unrealistic glossy finish, and often in colors that range from grotesque to unpleasant. Painting your own figures ensures that your miniature people will have the look you want.

Painting figures is also economical: A box of six decorated Preiser figures costs about $8, while a set of 120 unpainted Preiser figures is only $20. With a bit of effort you can populate a layout inexpensively, and have much better-looking scale people.

The HO scale Preiser people in fig. 1 are from set no. 16337. The figures come several to a sprue, and the sprue makes a handy handle for painting. Begin by cleaning any flash or mold lines with a knife as fig. 2 shows. When that's done, scrub the figures with warm water and dish detergent and let them dry.

Painting basics

I like to use water-based paints, as they don't present the problems of odor and hazardous vapors of solvent paints.

If you have an airbrush, spray the entire sprue of figures with a flesh color. If not, use a no. 0 or finer brush to paint the face, hands, and other exposed skin. For Caucasian skin I usually start with a Polly S mix of 2 parts no. 500810 Desert Pink and 1 part 410011 Reefer White. For African-American skin, mix Polly S 410010 Engine Black with 410070 Roof Brown and Desert Pink to create various shades. If you're airbrushing, thin this mixture with 40 percent Polly S Airbrush Thinner. These paints dry flat, which provides a good base for succeeding clothing colors.

You can give individual figures suntans and varying skin tones by varying the mix of white and pink or by adding a bit of no. 500014 Grimy Black to the mixture. You can also give figures a light coat of thinned Grimy Black (7 parts thinner, 1 part paint) applied with either an airbrush or with a brush as a wash. If an effect just doesn't turn out the way you want, simply paint more flesh color over it.

Use a fine-point brush (I like the Testor's Model Master no. 0 synthetic) to paint

Figures can help turn a bunch of objects into a bustling scene.

individual details as fig. 3 shows. Once again, use water-based flat colors. Paints with a creamy consistency are the easiest to work with. Polly S and Pactra Acrylic Enamel flats both work well, as do craft paints (Delta Ceramcoat is one brand).

Keep your brush wet with paint, and push the paint carefully up to the raised lines that define edges of clothing. If you go over an edge, don't worry – simply touch it up later.

Make sure clothing colors and styles are consistent with the era you're modeling. For example, the woman with the Nike logo on her shoes in fig. 1 wouldn't be appropriate before the mid-1970s. Solid-color clothes are the easiest to paint. Stripes and patterns are challenging, but are possible if you have a steady hand.

Final touches

When you're done with the clothing, use a knife to separate the figure from the sprue, clean up the head, then paint the hair. For blond hair use a mix of yellow, white, and brown, and vary the color among figures. For darker hair you can use any color from black to light brown.

I've found the best way for highlighting lips and eyebrows is with a pencil as shown in fig. 4. It's impossible to control paint in such a small area, and these details should be subtle. Trying to paint these details with a brush, even in O scale, usually results in a clown face. A standard graphite pencil works well for most figures, but you can use a red pencil for lipstick on female figures.

These techniques work well in any scale, even N, as shown in fig. 5. Since painting figures takes a bit of time, save your best efforts for foreground scenes where your miniature people are readily visible. Great detail isn't needed for figures in background scenes or large groups.

There's a good variety of figures available, but it's also possible to modify figures to adapt them to specific scenes or situations. By using a razor saw or knife to cut off an arm so you can reposition it, you can give a figure a new look. When doing this, be sure joints look natural – remember that the limbs should only bend at the joints.

A few additional tips:

• If a figure has a base, use a razor saw to slice it off just below the feet.

• Secure figures using a bit of Walthers Goo or a touch of glue from a glue stick.

• Place figures so they look natural – don't have a figure gesturing to an open space.

Armed with a handful of unpainted figures and a bit of patience, you'll have your layout populated in no time. ☼

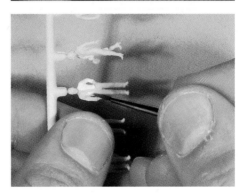

Fig. 2 CLEANING FLASH. Use a sharp knife to clean any flash from the back and extremities.

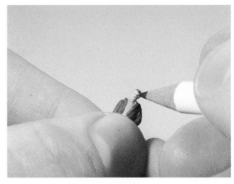

Fig. 3 CLOTHES. Brush paint to the ridges that define the boundaries between clothing.

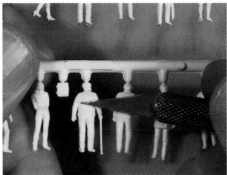

Fig. 4 FACIAL DETAILS. Add lips, eyebrows, and eye detail using an ordinary pencil.

Fig. 5 OTHER SCALES. Although more detail is possible in larger scales, it's easy to paint even N scale figures, such as the one at right, as well as her HO scale companion.

Making vehicles more realistic

Paint and detail tips for improving the looks of model cars

BY JEFF WILSON
PHOTOS BY REBECCA SALITURE

Vehicles are very important in helping set your layout's era. Although most people can't tell the difference between a 1963 Ford and a 1965 Ford, most have a good idea of what a mid-1960s car looks like as opposed to a 1970s or 1990s auto. Vehicles can also be nice models worthy of attention in their own right.

Fortunately, modelers in HO scale have a wide variety of vehicles available to them, and selections in N and other scales are growing. For an idea of what's available, check out your local hobby shop or the Walthers catalog.

Many of the nicer models, such as the Busch vehicles in the photo above, include headlights and taillights, interior details, chrome trim and hubcaps, mirrors, and grills. These are beautiful models that are essentially ready to place on the layout, but they're also relatively expensive – often $10 to $15 each.

Unless your budget allows, the most practical idea is usually to have a few of the nicer cars for foreground scenes but populate your layout's streets, highways, and parking lots with less expensive models. Many of these vehicles can be made much better with a bit of paint and an added detail or two.

Improving models

Figure 1 shows how I fixed up vehicles from Bachmann, Con-Cor, Eko, and Magnuson. Here are a few basic ideas:

It's usually easiest if you can disassemble the cars as much as possible. Wheels and grills are easier to paint if they're separate, and if you're planning to repaint the entire car it helps to get the clear plastic glazing out of the way.

Wheels are often molded solid black. Using a fine-point brush and some silver paint (I like Testor's no. 1146), paint the hubcaps, grills, door handles, and headlights (if they're just molded plastic). Paint a bit of silver where the taillights go. When that dries, add gloss red paint over it – the silver base will make the red brighter.

License plates are another nice touch, and the photo above shows several cars and trucks

KEY TO PHOTO, LEFT

1. Magnuson Models 1953 Chevrolet, cast polyurethane kit. Airbrushed Accu-Flex Louisville & Nashville Blue and Antique White.
2. Eko 1960s Ford Zephyr, assembled plastic model.
3. Bachmann mid-1970s Lincoln, assembled plastic model. Brush-painted Modelflex Gloss Blue over Primer Gray.
4. Con-Cor mid-1980s Ford Mustang, assembled plastic model.
5. Alloy Forms 1956 Ford pickup, cast-metal kit. Airbrushed Accu-Flex Engine Black.
6. Busch 1953 Chevrolet pickup (exclusive run for Euro-Rails Model Importers), assembled plastic model.
7. Williams Bros. 1940 Ford coupe, undecorated plastic kit. Airbrushed Accu-Flex Chicago & North Western Green.
8. Magnuson Models 1953 Ford tow truck, cast polyurethane kit. Airbrushed Accu-Flex Reefer Orange.
9. Busch (Euro-Rails) 1990s Chevrolet Caprice police car, assembled plastic model.

Fig. 1 BEFORE AND AFTER. The Eko Ford (lower right), Con-Cor Mustang (lower left), and Bachmann car (upper left) received painted grills, headlights, hubcaps, and taillights. The Mustang now also has a driver. The Eko and Bachmann cars had flash trimmed from the sides and wheel wells, and the Bachmann car received a new paint job with Modelflex Gloss Blue. The Magnuson tank truck is airbrushed white and green, with black behind the grill.

Fig. 2 CAST-METAL KITS. These N scale kits from GHQ – an unassembled Chevy crew-cab pickup at left and an assembled and painted Ford F-150 at right – show the fine detail that's becoming available on more and more model vehicles.

with them. Microscale makes two HO scale license plate decal sets: nos. MC-4168 (60-4168 for N scale) for commercial vehicles and MC-4149 (60-4149 for N) for standard cars and pickups.

Figures are another good detail. I added a driver to the Con-Cor Mustang shown in the lead photo and fig. 1. Preiser makes a set of seated figures, set no. 10090, but most any figure will work – simply cut the figure off just above the waist to get it to fit.

Kits

Simple plastic kits, like the HO models from Williams Bros., are a good place to start. The 1940 Ford in the big photo was molded in white plastic, but many of Williams' other vehicles are molded in clear styrene. Place pieces of masking tape over the windshield, window, and headlight areas, then paint these cars with an airbrush or spray can.

A hint on painting: Although it's possible to brush-paint vehicles, the easiest way to paint them is with an airbrush or spray can. Spray in light coats – two or three light coats are better than one heavy coat. If you must brush-paint, stick to dark colors. Use a soft, wide brush and as few strokes as possible to avoid brush marks. The Bachmann car in fig. 1 is one example.

If you're painting a model with dark colors, such as black or dark blues or greens, usually no primer is necessary. For light colors it's a good idea to paint the model first with a light base coat, such as gray.

Urethane kits, like Magnuson's, are usually molded in solid blocks, some of which (especially trucks) have two or more parts that need to be glued together. Start by using a hobby knife to remove any "flash," the stray material found around wheel wells and around the bottom edges of the casting. Smooth any rough areas with needle files or fine sandpaper. Glue the pieces together using gap-filling cyanoacrylate adhesive (CA) or five-minute epoxy.

The next step is extremely important. Before painting the model, scrub it thoroughly in warm water with dish detergent. Use an old toothbrush to get into all the nooks and crannies. This will clean the surface and get rid of any remaining mold-release compound.

Cast-metal vehicles are often the most difficult kits to assemble, although some – like the N scale GHQ pickup in fig. 2 – feature very clean castings. Clean up the castings with needle files and glue parts together with CA.

Windshields are always a challenge on solid cast-resin and cast-metal vehicles. The best paint I've found for this is Testor's no. 1539 Sapphire. It's a high-gloss, metallic blue color that comes about as close as possible to the look of sky reflected in glass. I used it on the Magnuson tow truck and 1953 Chevy in the lead photo, and associate editor Marty McGuirk used it on the GHQ pickup truck in fig. 2.

That's all it takes – you're now ready to give your layout's residents some classy wheels to cruise around in. ⚙

Rebecca Saliture

If your model citizens drive on unrealistic roads, perhaps it's time to start a highway improvement project.

Roads and grade crossings

Making realistic highways from sheet styrene

BY MARTY McGUIRK

Roads and highways are important to just about any layout because they add life and a sense of action. They also help set the layout's theme, its time, and place. And the best part is it's easy to make realistic and good-looking roads and grade crossings.

Model roads

All sorts of materials have been used to make roads including cardstock, cork, plaster, and even real tar. Some manufacturers offer ready-made roads. In HO scale, Walthers offers city streets, sidewalks, and a modern grade crossing. For N scalers, Fine N Scale (1517 Via Boronada, Palos Verdes, CA 90274; 310-373-6658) has an assortment of sidewalks and curbs.

Styrene highway

My favorite material for modeling paved roads is styrene because it's smooth, flexible,

and easy to work with. For this article I built a short stretch of road atop a foam board surface, but styrene roads can also be built directly over existing scenery.

Once you know the path the road will follow, draw two lines at least 24 scale feet apart. This will give you two 12-foot lanes, which are ideal for layouts set in the 1950s.

Next, cut a piece of .030" plain sheet styrene 24 scale feet wide. Straight roads like mine are easy, but it's not hard to cut curves into the styrene. If you're building a long road, hide any seams between individual styrene sections with filler or start with a large sheet. (Styrene is sold in 4 x 8-foot sheets at most plastic supply houses.) I used two pieces of styrene, trimming to match the angle of the track.

The crossing

Before attaching the road to the foam board I built the crossing. Crossings vary widely, depending on the era you model. Early crossings were dirt piled between the rails. Later, wooden planks were added. Pavement, with timbers on either side of the rail like the example in fig. 1, is also common. Today, steel plates or hard rubber mats are common. My layout is set in the 1950s, so I prefer wooden crossings.

I used Kappler Kontour HO scale ties. Use cyanoacrylate adhesive (CA) to attach several ties to the outside edge of both rails the full width of the road. To get these level with the top of the rails, I added a .030" styrene shim between the Kappler ties and the plastic ties on my Atlas flextrack. Then I added the planks between the rails, staggering the ends (fig. 2) so the joints weren't next to one another.

Run a car through the crossing to make sure couplers and wheels pass without interference. Prototype wooden crossings have angles cut in the ends of the boards to help any dragging equipment pass up and over. I angled the ties with a sharp hobby knife and then stained them Floquil Maple.

On the road again

Secure the styrene road to the surface of the layout with latex Liquid Nails. After the cement has set overnight, scribe expansion joints into the styrene every 12 feet. I also like to add jagged cracks with the hobby knife. Add a lot of cracks and the road will appear older and neglected; fewer cracks reflect a newer or better maintained roadway. See fig. 3.

When that's done, blend the edges of the road into the surrounding area with Sculptamold or plaster, paying special attention to any gaps caused by the road climbing to track level.

Finishing touches

I painted the road with Testor's Accu-Flex 16-99 Flat Dull Gray. Paint your road any medium gray color, but stay away from jet black. It's almost impossible to make a black road look realistic under indoor lighting, and only a brand-new asphalt road ever looks black anyway.

All sorts of crossing signals are available, ranging from crossbucks to operating gates and flashers. I added a crossing flasher set and a yellow RR crossing sign, both from N. J. International. You can make the gates and flashers operate, but that's beyond the scope of this article.

Weathering (fig. 4) is needed to bring out the detail you scribed into the styrene. Apply a generous quantity of powdered black and pastel chalk directly to the road and use a soft brush to spread it over the surface. Then use your finger to remove the chalk from both sides of the traffic lanes, leaving dark streaks down the centers.

I use Post-It notes to mask the traffic lanes, applying Reefer White paint directly to the road using a dabbing motion (fig. 5). As a general rule, model railroads set in an earlier era should have fewer markings on the streets than modern-era layouts. I added a center line to my road and a stop line before the crossing.

Probably the best advice I can offer is this: Next time you're out driving, notice the variations and details found on any street. Then try to incorporate those into your layout. ✿

David Plowden

Fig. 1 PROTOTYPE GRADE CROSSING. Grade crossings have changed since this photo was taken in Brattleboro, Vt., in 1955. Note the paved crossing with timbers on each side of the rails, the manual gates, and the crossing shanty.

Fig. 2 PLANKED CROSSING. Use CA to secure "Kontour" HO scale ties to the plastic ties between and alongside the rails. Test-run a freight car through the crossing before gluing anything down!

Fig. 3 ADDING CRACKS AND JOINTS. Use a sharp hobby knife to scribe expansion joints and cracks into the surface of the road. Don't get too carried away with this step!

Fig. 4 WEATHERING. The painted road and finished scenery look okay, but the road lacks texture. Adding powdered chalk takes care of that.

Fig. 5 STRIPING. Mask off the areas to be lined and use a stiff brush to dab on the paint. The fall trees were made using Jane's Trains of Texas Forest in a Flash kits.

Modeling photos by the author

We build the Alkali Central: 1

A 4x8 HO layout featuring mountain and desert scenery

BY JIM KELLY

The HO layout you see on these next few pages was built by the MODEL RAILROADER staff with lots of help from our friends in other departments here at Kalmbach Publishing. You can see most of their happy faces in fig. 1. It's no coincidence we're presenting the layout in our December issue, as every year that's the issue picked up by thousands of newcomers to the hobby. Lots of them are looking for information on getting started, and we always try to oblige. One way to cover a lot of the basics quickly is to show how to build a small layout step by step. We call these layouts project railroads, and over the years we've featured dozens of them.

We built the Alkali Central in HO scale, simply because that's far and away the most popular size and the choice of 75 percent of our readers. Also we built it on a table made from a 4 x 8-foot sheet of plywood because that's such a readily available, strong, and inexpensive material.

The AC is small and simple, but we think it has lots of interesting operating potential. It's really two railroads in one, the Southern Pacific and the AC. Headquartered in Alkali Junction, where it interchanges with the SP, the AC runs 23 miles out into the Alkali Desert to a phosphate mine. The backdrop down the middle of the layout gives us the opportunity to model two kinds of scenery – California foothills on one side and raw desert on the other.

Photos of completed layout: Chris Becker

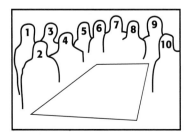

Fig. 1 THE ALKALI CENTRAL BUILDERS

1. Jeff Wilson	Associate editor, MR	Track, wiring, gas station, details
2. Jim Hediger	Senior editor, MR	Benchwork
3. Erik Bergstrom	Ad sales representative, MR	Grain elevator, ballast
4. Mike Danneman	Art Director, *Trains* Magazine	Backdrop painting, details
5. Art Curren	Production coordinator	Phosphate mine
6. Mike Brickl	Ad services representative	Ballast
7. Jim Kelly	Managing editor, MR	Scenery, station
8. Barb Packenham	Editorial assistant, MR	Rix houses, scenery
9. Marty McGuirk	Assoc. editor, *Classic Toy Trains*	Tavern
10. Keith Thompson	Associate editor, MR	Structures, scenery, details

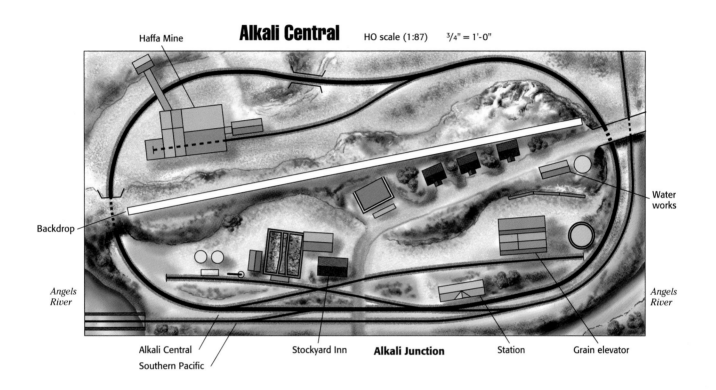

Alkali Central   HO scale (1:87)   ³/₄" = 1'-0"

Haffa Mine

Water works

Backdrop

Angels River

Angels River

Alkali Central
Southern Pacific

Stockyard Inn   **Alkali Junction**   Station   Grain elevator

One side of the HO layout features Alkali Junction, a fictional California foothill town of the early '50s. The mighty Southern Pacific stops here to interchange cars with the Alkali Central, known locally as "the Desert Rat." The "Rat" picked up its 2-6-0 Mogul cheap from the SP. It's an IHC model, fortunately following an SP prototype.

Fig. 2 BENCHWORK. We wanted the table to have a rustic look, so we roughed it up with a belt sander. The inset photo shows how the tops of the legs form tabs that project up into pockets in the tabletop. Gravity does the rest.

Bill of materials, benchwork
4 12-foot 1 x 4s
4 8-foot 1 x 3s
2 8-foot 1 x 2s
2 4 x 8 sheets, ½" plywood
1 18" x 6'-8" interior door
2 6" angle iron braces
1 box 1½" drywall screws
9 ¼" x 2" carriage bolts
8 ¼" nuts
1 ¼" wingnut

The benchwork

Jim Hediger built the benchwork, shown in fig. 2. He attributes its innovative design to his days as a Boy Scouts leader, as it borrows from a trestle-table design used for Scout projects. Those who've given it the jiggle test have been amazed at how solid this table is. We also like it because it's interesting, attractive, and makes the layout easy to move. You can lift the tabletop off the leg assembly, then disassemble the base into flat pieces for easy transport.

Figure 3 shows how to build the tabletop. Jim cut all the wood with an electric saber saw. Assembling the top is really a job for two, so you'll probably need a helper. C-clamps are also handy when it comes time to add the 2 x 2 corner blocks and the 1 x 2 corner braces.

Jim joined the pieces with carpenter's glue and drywall screws, zipping them in with a Phillips screwdriver bit in an electric drill. You should drill pilot holes for any screws going near the ends of boards to avoid splitting the wood.

To support our western theme we wanted the boards to look a bit old and worn, an effect Jim accomplished with an electric belt sander. You could do the same with a utility knife and sandpaper – it would just take longer.

Jim says it's easier to build a basic table top and then go back and fit in the riverbeds than it is to plan for these in advance. Working them in calls for careful cutting with the saber saw, angling the blade when coming to the framing boards so as not to cut too deeply into them. The "minus" dimensions on the drawing are to the top of the water.

Legs and backdrop

Figure 4 shows how the leg assembly was made. Cutting the curves into the support panels was a cosmetic touch you could leave out. Keith held a bent yardstick against the plywood while Jim traced the curve. Then Jim made the first cut-out and used it as a pattern for the others. The belt sander made short work of smoothing the edges.

Once the benchwork was finished, Jim stained it, let it dry overnight, then sealed the surfaces with a clear polyurethane finish.

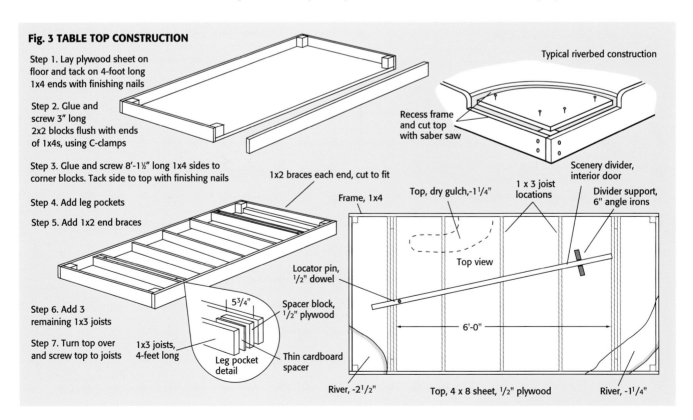

Fig. 3 TABLE TOP CONSTRUCTION

Step 1. Lay plywood sheet on floor and tack on 4-foot long 1x4 ends with finishing nails

Step 2. Glue and screw 3" long 2x2 blocks flush with ends of 1x4s, using C-clamps

Step 3. Glue and screw 8'-1½" long 1x4 sides to corner blocks. Tack side to top with finishing nails

Step 4. Add leg pockets

Step 5. Add 1x2 end braces

Step 6. Add 3 remaining 1x3 joists

Step 7. Turn top over and screw top to joists

Typical riverbed construction

Recess frame and cut top with saber saw

Scenery divider, interior door

Divider support, 6" angle irons

1x2 braces each end, cut to fit

Frame, 1x4

Top, dry gulch,-1¼"

1 x 3 joist locations

Top view

Locator pin, ½" dowel

Spacer block, ½" plywood

5¾"

1x3 joists, 4-feet long

Leg pocket detail

Thin cardboard spacer

6'-0"

River, -2½"

Top, 4 x 8 sheet, ½" plywood

River, -1¼"

Using a prefab interior door for a backdrop was Keith Thompson's idea, and it worked out very well. We chose one with a birch skin for its smooth surface. Less expensive doors, sheathed with lauan plywood, would take a lot of filling and sanding to eliminate coarse grain. Jim Hediger installed the door so that a hole in the edge at one end drops over an alignment pin made from a 1/2" dowel. The other end drops between a pair of 6" angle irons screwed to the table. We didn't get around to painting the backdrop until after we'd built the scenery, but you'd just as well paint yours right at the get-go.

Laying out the track plan

We built the AC with Atlas track because it's a good brand that's widely available and most model railroaders get started with it. As the track plan shows, we used a combination of sectional and flexible track. Sectional track offers one big advantage: It's hard to make mistakes, particularly when you're laying curves. Still, you should work carefully, and one of the most critical stages comes before you've laid any track at all. You need to do a particularly good job of laying the plan out on the table top.

The most accurate way of doing this is to use the track pieces themselves. Fit them together and trace along their edges, as shown in fig. 5. You can use the edge of an index card to tick off the track centerline, then drill a hole for a pencil in a yard stick and swing it like a big compass to draw the curves. Obviously you can use that same yardstick to draw center lines for the straight sections. The minimum curve radius is supposed to be 18", so this is an excellent time to make certain it is.

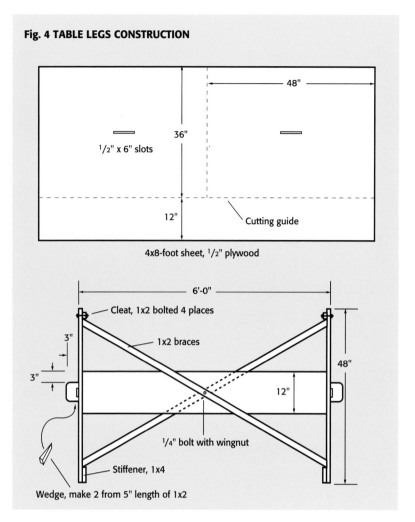

Fig. 4 TABLE LEGS CONSTRUCTION

48"

36"

1/2" x 6" slots

12"

Cutting guide

4x8-foot sheet, 1/2" plywood

6'-0"

Cleat, 1x2 bolted 4 places

3"

1x2 braces

3"

48"

12"

1/4" bolt with wingnut

Stiffener, 1x4

Wedge, make 2 from 5" length of 1x2

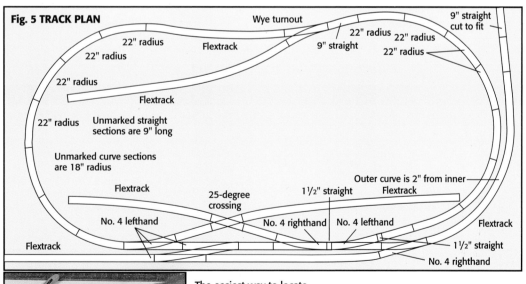

Fig. 5 TRACK PLAN

Wye turnout

9" straight cut to fit

22" radius

Flextrack

22" radius

9" straight

22" radius 22" radius

22" radius

22" radius

22" radius

Flextrack

22" radius   Unmarked straight sections are 9" long

Unmarked curve sections are 18" radius

Flextrack

Outer curve is 2" from inner

25-degree crossing

1 1/2" straight   Flextrack

No. 4 lefthand

No. 4 righthand   No. 4 lefthand

Flextrack

Flextrack

1 1/2" straight

No. 4 righthand

The easiest way to locate the track is to lay the actual components on the table and trace their outlines with a pencil. You can tack the pieces temporarily with a few track nails.

Bill of materials, track
Atlas
55 insulating plastic rail joiners
168 flextrack, 7
172 Custom-Line 25-degree crossing
280 Custom-Line wye turnout
281 Custom-Line no. 4 lefthand turnouts, 3
282 Custom-Line no. 4 right-hand turnouts, 2
842 nickel silver terminal joiners
170 nickel silver rail joiners

Midwest
Cork roadbed, 3-foot strips, 14

One side of the layout features the Alkali Desert and this phosphate mine built by Art Curren, kitbasher extraordinaire. Art calls it Haffa Mine because he used about half of a Walthers coal mine kit.

Fig. 6 CORK ROADBED. Step one is laying the first half-strip along the track center line, going right on through any turnouts you come to. We cement the cork with a bead of yellow glue.

The opposite side strip has been added. It butts the first in the right side of the photo but follows the center line of the turnout's diverging route. Now we're finishing the curved leg by cutting down through the cork and trimming it to fit.

To finish the straight route off the turnout we trim another piece of cork, cutting straight down through it and notching the lower piece for a good fit. Lightly sanding the top of the cork will keep the track even.

Cork roadbed

Figure 6 shows how we laid the cork roadbed, again, the modeler's most popular choice. "Why use roadbed at all?" you might ask. You can get by without it, but it makes a model railroad look more like the real thing by representing the stone bed (called ballast) that supports the ties. (Eventually we'll add a thin layer of miniature stone over this to make it look more real.)

The cork comes in 3-foot long strips split nearly through down the middle at a 45-degree angle. You simply peel the strips in two and butt the 90-degree edges together. Now you know why you needed to draw that track centerline. Laying the cork for turnouts gets a little tricky, and fig. 6 also shows how.

We've seen a lot of overkill when it comes to laying cork roadbed. You don't need a nail every few inches, and in fact you don't really need nails at all. Just lay down a bead of yellow carpenters glue, press the roadbed down on it, and it'll grab in about 30 seconds. Sometimes we'll use a nail or two near the end of a curved piece to hold it so we can keep on going. Even then we drive it only partly in and pull it out later.

Laying the track

One secret to good track laying is making sure the pieces fit properly. You're just asking for trouble if you try to force them, so take your time and make sure you have smooth transitions from one section of track to the next. You may have to trim rail ends where gaps are excessive, as shown in fig. 7.

Rail joiners should slide on smoothly, and if they don't, something's wrong. Usually it's burrs on rail ends, even if these were cut at the factory. You may not be able to see them, but the

Fig. 7 LAYING TRACK. It's vital that track pieces fit properly. Don't force them. A slight gap is good, but it shouldn't exceed 1/16". If it does, mark the excess.

Trim the rail with rail nippers. Good ones will make track laying so much easier, and it's a good idea not to use them for cutting anything else.

Dress the cut ends with a file so rail joiners will slip on readily. They provide both a mechanical and an electrical connection so should fit snugly.

Once the track fits, nail it in place, using Atlas track nails. Use a nail set to carefully seat the nails. The nail heads should barely contact the ties.

This nail is driven in too far, distorting the tie and drawing the railheads closer together. This could contribute to derailments, especially on curves.

rail joiner knows they're there. You can fix this problem easily with a few strokes of a file.

By now you may have noticed there's nothing in the turnouts to hold the moving point rails against the stationary stock rails. Figure 8 shows how Keith Thompson solved this with a simple toggle spring. We just throw turnouts "digitally" (with our fingers), and the springs hold them in position.

Wiring

Figure 5 also shows how Jeff Wilson wired the layout. He included three short on-off sections where engines can be parked. These are controlled by simple single-pole, single-throw toggle switches mounted in the edge of the layout. You can buy appropriate switches at Radio Shack or other electronics stores. The idea is this: The Alkali Central steam engine can be parked by the oil tanks with that track section shut off. Then the Southern Pacific diesel can roll forward into Alkali Junction, set off cars, then move onto the bridge or under the highway bridge, where the power to it can be shut off. The power to the AC engine can then be turned on and it can go to work.

So much for theory. None of this can happen, though, until you connect feeder wires to the track. An easy way to do so is with Atlas no. 842 terminal joiners. These are simply rail joiners with a pair of feeder wires already soldered to them. See fig. 9.

The power pack Jeff chose is the Chicago Model International Hogger Blue, and he picked it because of its walkaround and memory features. Since the layout features a backdrop down the middle we wanted to be able to unplug the throttle, walk around to the other side, and plug it back in again.

Making the train run

At this point you should be able to run a train. If you can't it's probably because the track isn't clean. For a small layout like this you can't beat a Bright Boy track cleaner. This is an abrasive block you can buy at the hobby shop.

Now's a good time to just kick back and enjoy running the trains. See you again next month when we'll add scenery and structures, then have one of our favorite artists show us how to paint a backdrop. ✿

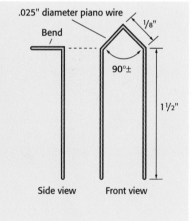

Fig. 8 TURNOUT TOGGLES. These simple homemade springs hold the turnout points firmly against the stock rails, yet the points can be easily thrown with just a flick of the fingertip.

.025" diameter piano wire
1/8"
Bend
90°±
1 1/2"
Side view   Front view

Fig. 9 WIRING. Jeff Wilson built this simple plywood shelf under the layout to support the power pack. The walkaround throttles plug into telephone jacks on the side of the layout.

Atlas terminal rail joiners have feeder wires attached, making electrical connections easy. Just drill a hole next to the joiner, poke the wires through, and connect them to the power pack.

We build the Alkali Central: 2

Scenery, structures, and details bring our layout to life

BY JIM KELLY

Last month we introduced our HO scale layout, the Alkali Central. It's a 4 x 8-foot model railroad following a western theme and featuring a California foothills town on one side of the backdrop and a desert scene on the other. Now that the trains are running, it's time to add scenery, structures, and details to bring that sheet of plywood to life. Whether you're building the Alkali Central or some other railroad these are basic techniques you can use, regardless of the scale you're modeling in.

Cardboard web scenery

There are lots of good ways to build hills and mountains on a layout. For a good rundown we recommend Dave Frary's book *How to Build Realistic Model Railroad Scenery*, published by our parent company, Kalmbach Publishing Co. For the Alkali Central I was the landscaper and used the cardboard strip method, as shown in fig. 1. This is inexpensive, goes quite quickly, and the shapes you form are easily controlled and modified.

You'll need some 1"-wide strips of corrugated cardboard. One large shipping carton, say for a television set, will provide all you need, and you can slice them off with a utility knife.

Also you'll need two different kinds of heavy-duty staplers, one for driving staples into the plywood and a pliers type for stapling strips together. You can also do the job with a hot glue gun.

Let the photos be your guide. Naturally your scenery isn't going to come out exactly like mine, and there's no reason it should.

You can change the contours easily by cutting strips and re-stapling the ends closer together, or by splicing in new strips to move them farther apart.

Engine no. 522, an IHC Mogul, glides around Rattlesnake Hill in our desert scene. We cast the plaster rocks in latex rubber molds, as shown in fig. 3.

Adding the hardshell

Having built a skeleton, now you need to add some skin. As shown in fig. 2, I used Rigid-Wrap, a plaster-impregnated gauze. It comes in a 4"-wide roll and you simply cut off strips about 8" long, dip them in water, and lay them on your cardboard web form. I know of no other method that's as mess-free as this. Woodland Scenics also offers the same sort of material.

Once this hardshell has set – give it 24 hours – you can start building up the ground. On the AC I used Sculptamold, a lightweight material similar to paper-mache that again is very controllable and easy to work with. I like to brush it on quickly with a cheap 1" brush, let it set a few minutes, and then start smoothing and working it with the same brush dipped in water. The layer is about 1/4" to 1/2" thick and at this stage you're working to hide the grid pattern in the hardshell caused by the underlying cardboard web as well as any unnatural hollows.

Rock smithing

Figure 3 shows how I made the rocks using rubber molds. You'll need three or four. Several manufacturers make these and you can buy them at hobby shops. Inexpensive molding plaster, patching plaster, or plaster of paris are all good for making rocks and one 5-pound bag or box will provide all you need for a small layout like the AC.

Dip your molds in water, then fill them with plaster of paris and let them start setting up. For lack of a better metaphor you want the plaster about the consistency of catsup, but not that real slow-pouring kind.

Photos of finished layout: Chris Becker

The Alkali Central's Desert Rat rolls into town just in time to catch a glimpse of the Southern Pacific pulling out. The AC engine is a Southern Pacific 2-6-0 Mogul by IHC and runs very well.

Fig. 1 CARDBOARD WEB SCENERY. We wove cardboard strips together to build hills. The blue paper kept scenery materials from sticking to the backdrop, as we wanted it to be removable.

We used a pliers-type stapler to fasten the strips where they crossed. The angle iron seen on the right is matched by one on the opposite side of the backdrop and holds the backdrop in position.

Fig. 2 ADDING THE HARDSHELL. We draped our hills with Rigid Wrap, a plaster-impregnated gauze that you just dip in water and position. A double layer will give plenty of strength.

Once the gauze shell had set hard we applied Sculptamold with a putty knife. This is a lightweight scenery product that works easily without the mess of plaster and gives you plenty of working time.

We used a throwaway 1" brush dipped in water to smooth the Sculptamold. In photos of the desert side you can spot some erosion lines we worked in with the brush and a large screwdriver.

Our Southern Pacific GP7 is an Athearn model. The SP had no GP7s, but its virtually identical GP9s spelled doom for the SP's Moguls. Fortunately, one of them found a home on the Alkali Central.

Fig. 3 MODELING ROCKS. We cast our rocks by pouring soupy plaster in rubber molds. As soon as the plaster crinkles when you flex the mold it's time to wet the scenery and apply the casting.

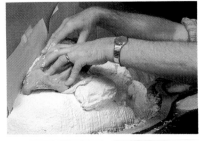

We'll hold the mold against the rock until the plaster grabs, which usually takes only a few minutes. Resist the temptation to pull the mold off for at least an hour or you'll wreck the fine detail.

Keep your eye on the molds and test them now and then by flexing them. When the plaster starts losing its watery shine and the surface crinkles, you're ready to place the mold on the layout. Make sure to liberally spray the area first with water so the dry Sculptamold won't suck the water out of the casting and ruin it.

Plaster is not real predictable stuff. Sometimes it'll start to set in 3 or 4 minutes, and sometimes it takes 15 or 20. One advantage is that it's cheap, so if you suffer some failures you can just throw them away.

Painting the rocks

Next I painted the rocks, using artist's tube acrylics purchased at an art supply store. The

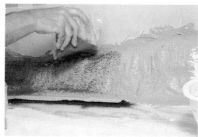

Fig. 4 COLORING THE SCENERY. We painted the scenery with an inexpensive flat tan latex paint thinned about 50:50 with water. It provided color and also served as an adhesive.

Next we sprinkled on texture materials, using various sand and dirt products as well as ground foam. Representing a barren desert or lush, green fields is simply a matter of the materials used.

As the texture built up we sprayed the scenery with dilute matte medium, thoroughly soaking it, then added more texture and sprayed again, building up until we were pleased with the result.

Fig. 5 PLANTING STRUCTURES. We built our hill first, then recontoured it with a hammer. Squares of 3/16" foam core board made good homesites. We leveled them with wetted paper wads before covering them with plaster gauze and Sculptamold.

Here's the brick station platform being installed on pieces of .060" styrene. We used the plastic brick sheet because the builder lost the platform parts that came in the kit. We used a Master Creations kit, but lots of others could be substituted.

Keith Thompson was our bridge man. He has a neat method for installing them by cementing them to the track with Goo adhesive and tying them in place temporarily with twist ties. Then he works the abutments into position from underneath.

brand was Liquitex, although there are plenty of other good quality brands out there. I used only three colors: burnt umber, burnt sienna, and white.

To do likewise spray water on the rocks to help the paint flow, then squeeze an inch or two of each color out on a plate, a jar lid, a palette or whatever, dip a flat ½" brush in water, then into color, and go to work. I like to flow a dark color (in this case burnt umber) on first and get it to run into the crevices. You can spray it with water to get it to run around.

You can then start mixing lighter shades of brown by dipping your brush into the different colors and brushing them on. The main point is to keep the paint fairly thin. You'll be surprised at how well you can do and how quickly you'll discover various effects. Also, you can quit anytime and return to try other effects later.

After the rocks have dried for several days you can make them really "pop" by lightly drybrushing them with light colors and even a little white. A ½" flat brush works well. Dip the tip lightly into the paint, then wipe the brush off on a rag. Stroke the rocks lightly, working vertically, and a trace of paint will appear on the high spots. Go easy, less is more.

Coloring and texturing the ground

Figure 4 shows how I added color and texture to the ground. The first step was painting it with flat tan latex paint thinned about 50:50 with water. This adds color and also serves as an adhesive for the first layer of scenery.

After that it was a matter of sprinkling on scenery materials. On the desert side I used Highball Earth and various other sands and dirts sold in bags at the hobby shop.

For foliage I used ground foam by Woodland Scenics and others. This is simply foam rubber that has been ground to various grades and dyed various shades of green. For the most natural results you need to leave some bare or near-bare spots here and there. Also you need to use several shades and textures of green.

Build up the foliage in layers, spraying it periodically with a dilute solution (6 parts water, 1 part medium) from a household spray bottle, available in hardware or garden stores. Add several drops of liquid dishwashing detergent to this mix to help it penetrate.

Planting buildings

In writing a story about building a model railroad we progress logically from one step to the next. The actual construction, however, doesn't proceed in such an orderly fashion. Figure 5, for example, shows how we built level lots for the row of houses after the hardshell hill was already in place. The photo also demonstrates the versatility of this scenery method. Making changes is a simple matter of carefully whacking the effected areas with a hammer and rebuilding with Rigid-Wrap and Sculptamold.

Fig. 6 MODELING WATER. For water we used a thin layer of black-painted Sculptamold on the plywood base. The tan colors of the shore were feathered out into it for a realistic transition. Here gloss medium is being brushed on to add shine.

Making waves

Barb Packenham modeled our rivers. First she spread a thin layer of Sculptamold onto the plywood; then she worked in some waves by dabbing at the Sculptamold with a paintbrush.

Once the water was completely dry she painted it with Accu-Flex Engine Black. After the black dried thoroughly she brushed on acrylic gloss medium, as shown in fig. 6.

"Black water?" I can hear some of you muttering. Strange as it may seem, it works. You're creating a shiny, reflective surface that the mind accepts as representing water.

Ballasting track

Figure 7 shows how we ballasted the track. We used Highball's gray on the SP main line and cinders on the AC to help reinforce the concept that these were two different railroads.

Ballasting is a job that takes care and patience, so don't try to do the whole railroad at once. Be

The Alkali Central's steam engine is an oil burner and is fueled from these twin tanks in Alkali Junction. The loading pen is owned by the Southern Pacific and serves small ranchers who still drive cattle 50 miles or more cross-country.

Fig. 7 BALLASTING TRACK. Step 1 is carefully distributing the ballast. Paper or plastic cups work fine. A soft 1" brush works well for smoothing it. Tapping lightly on the tracks with a brush handle also helps distribute the ballast evenly.

After carefully and thoroughly wetting the ballast with water from a spray bottle we dribbled on diluted matte medium. The ballast should be thoroughly saturated. Once the matte medium dries, the ballast will look natural but be firmly bonded.

Fig. 8 BACKDROP PAINTING. Before slinging paint Mike Danneman sketched his scenery with colored chalk. To get a further sense of forms and shadowing he rubbed the chalk in places with his fingers.

For closer hills he used the same tan paint we'd used for basic scenery painting; for hills farther back he lightened it. Adding blue also makes forms look farther away. Mike didn't try to add much detail.

Mike painted clouds on the foothills side of the layout, but left the skies clear on the desert side to enhance the contrast. Payne's gray is his favorite color to represent the darker undersides of the clouds.

Fig. 9 STRUCTURES

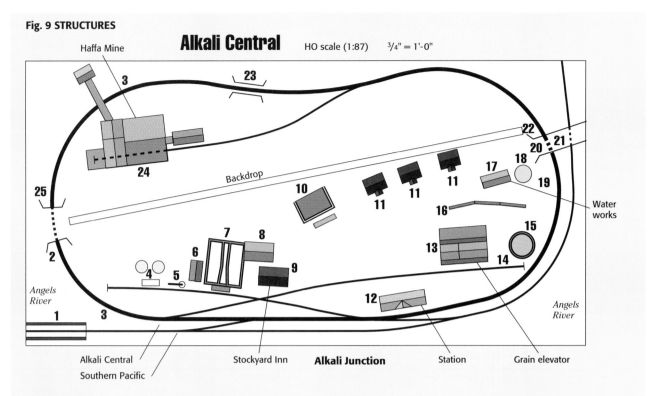

Alkali Central HO scale (1:87) $^3/_4$" = 1'-0"

Haffa Mine

23

22

20 21

3

17 18

24 19

25 Water works

10

11 11

11 11

16

15

2 7 8 13

6 14

Angels River 4 5 9

12

1 3

Alkali Central
Southern Pacific

Stockyard Inn **Alkali Junction** Station Grain elevator

Angels River

Backdrop

Structure key

1. Kibri 9694 girder bridge
2. Chooch 7020 and 7018 random stone wall and portal
3. Creative Model Assoc. 1004 telltale
4. Williams Bros. 501 storage tank kit
5. Creative Model Assoc. 1002 oil column
6. Campbell Scale Models 425 Kiowa trackside details no. 1
7. Life-Like 1378 stock pen
8. BH Models 502 Kirby Wagon Works
9. Grandt Line 5900 Second Chance Saloon

10. City Classics 108 1930s Crafton Avenue Service Station
11. Rix Products 203 one-story house w/side porch (3)
12. Master Creations 1400 station
13. American Model Builders 110 country grain elevator
14. Atlas 705 telephone shanty
15. Detail Associates 7004 Ponderosa water tank
16. A.I.M. Products 106 cut-stone retaining wall (cut down)
17. Vollmer 5612 workshop

18. Korber 125 70-foot 1960s vintage water tank (cut down)
19. Walthers 933-3133 plain billboard
20. Rix 106 roadway
21. Rix 101 vintage 50-foot highway overpass
22. Chooch 7039 cut-stone bridge abutments
23. Atlas 885 65-foot bridge
24. Walthers 933-3017 New River Mining Co.
25. Chooch 7003 "1901" concrete tunnel portal

content with a few feet at a time, at least until you get the hang of it, and stay away from the turnouts until you have gained some experience.

The first step is distributing the ballast along the track. If you haven't already done so, use coarse sandpaper to smooth the shoulders of the cork as roughness there makes the job surprisingly more difficult. Some modelers avoid ballasting around the moving points on turnouts altogether, but we don't. We're just very careful to use no more ballast than necessary.

Next wet the ballast, misting on water from a spray bottle. Add several drops of liquid dishwashing detergent to the water to help it soak in. If the water beads up and won't penetrate you need more detergent.

Next bond the ballast with diluted matte medium, the same brew you used on the scenery. Keep dribbling this on until the ballast is thoroughly soaked. Once the adhesive dries you'll see no sign of it. The ballast will look natural, but be firmly bonded in place.

Wrapping it up

Mike Danneman, art director of *Trains* Magazine, enjoys a national reputation for his railroad paintings, so we were delighted when he agreed to paint our backdrops. Figure 8 shows how he went about it. According to Mike, the key is not to strive for a lot of detail. Remember, this is the backdrop; it plays a subordinate role to the trains and the scenery up front.

Figure 9 includes a list of the structures we used on the layout. We built most of them "by the box." The one big exception is Art Curren's mine on the desert side, and we'll let him tell about that in his story beginning on the next page. Dozens of other kits could be substituted for the ones we used.

We couldn't cover every aspect of building the railroad in these two articles, but never fear, we'll keep the "Basic Model Railroading" articles coming. Meanwhile, we hope we've helped you get started on a layout of your own. We know you'll enjoy it. ☼

A. L. Schmidt

This 6-foot-long Ntrak module, the Breakneck Mountain, was built by several MODEL RAIL-ROADER staff members. Note the amount of scenery – a mountain, tunnel, river – and details that are packed into this module.

Modular railroading

No room for a layout? Here's another option

BY MELANIE GOHDE

Would you like to get started in model railroading but find that you have neither the space, time, nor money at this point for a full-fledged layout? Then perhaps you should consider building a module instead.

What's a module?

Let's start with a couple definitions. Having a sectional layout means you build your (or your club's) model railroad in several pieces that can be taken apart for easy portability. Each section will only fit in a specified place on that layout.

A module is constructed following a standard pattern or dimensions (usually length, width, height, and track position) and can be connected interchangeably with any other module built to the same standards. Typical modules are 4 to 8 feet long, 24" wide, 40" high with an 8" to 14" sky-board attached to the back, and have one or more tracks that will connect to another module.

After adhering to such standards, use your creativity. Your module can depict a desert, mountain, river, city, or anything else you'd like. You're also free to choose the buildings and figures and add as many details as you want. Can't pick just one theme to model? Build two modules, each with a different theme.

History

While people have been building sectional layouts since the beginning of model railroading, it wasn't until Ntrak was started in 1974 that uniform standards were developed for modules. When this group of California N scale modelers joined forces, their purpose was to get N scalers out of their garages and into National Model Railroad Association meets, therefore promoting the scale in public and encouraging development of N scale products. At the 1974 NMRA national convention, they ran a 12 x 72-foot N scale modular layout with 50- to 100- car trains running on the three-track, closed-loop layout.

Today thousands of Ntrak modules are operated by local clubs throughout the United States and Canada. Groups are also active in England, the Netherlands, Australia, and New Zealand. The organization publishes a manual of specifications, a bimonthly newsletter, plus other informational booklets.

However, modules aren't just for N scale anymore. Module clubs in just about every scale have cropped up. For example, a group of freestyle modular railroaders called *Fr*iends circle of *E*uropean *Mo*del railroaders, or FREMO, formed in 1981. It brings together nearly 600 modelers from all over Europe to operate single track, point-to-point layouts. FREMO, which started with HO modules, now uses N and O scales as well. You can contact them at P. O. Box 100 536, Darmstadt D-64205, Germany, or you can visit FREMO's World Wide Web site at http://ourworld.compuserve.com/homepages/shipmill/inhalt_e.htm.

Modules may be for you

Here are some reasons to consider taking up modular railroading:

• Limited space: You live in an apartment or a house with no extra room for a layout and don't have a basement.

• Move often: You're in the military or have another job that requires frequent relocation.

• Tangible accomplishment: A module completed in a short time can give you an immediate feeling of accomplishment that a large layout which takes years to complete may not.

• Developing skills: You'll learn about track planning, track laying, ballasting, scenery, and electronics on a small scale, giving you a chance to hone your skills before tackling a large layout. Knowing that you can complete a module may give you the confidence to start a layout.

• Limited resources: Because of your job or family situation you don't have a lot of time and/or money to spend on a large layout.

• New scale: You're an HO modeler with a layout in your basement, but you'd like to give N scale a try now that there are more products available. Without starting over on a new layout, you can try the new scale by incorporating your module into an Ntrak club layout and see how you like it with a minimal investment of time and money.

• Making the hobby public: You want to share this hobby (and display your work) with the public to encourage new modelers and promote model railroading. Modular layouts are often put together and run in shopping malls and at model shows.

• Club room: Your club can't find or afford a room in which to keep a permanent layout. If you find a place (or places) to gather occasionally, everyone brings their own module and you make a temporary layout and hold operating sessions. Also, your club layout isn't a lost cause if you lose your headquarters.

Getting started

If you'd like to build an N scale module, contact Ntrak Publishing, 1150 Wine Country Place, Templeton, CA 93465. See the August 1996 Workshop in MR for a listing of its publications, or visit Ntrak's Web site (http://www.mv.com:80/users/kgg/ntrak/).

The NMRA also has standards and recommended practices for modules. Contact them at 4121 Cromwell Rd., Chattanooga, TN 37421. The standards are published on the NMRA Web site (http://www.nmra.org).

To see an example of modules as layout design elements, read Bernard Kempinski's article "Planning a realistic layout using Ntrak modules" in *Model Railroad Planning* 1997, which goes on sale the first week in March.

There are several listings on the Internet of modular clubs. Ntrak's site has a club list, as does the site at http://ourworld.compuserve.com/homepages/Thomas_Murphy/nclub.htm, which includes club addresses plus some e-mail addresses and Web links for clubs worldwide. ☼

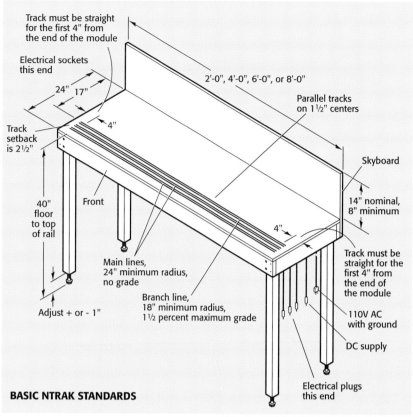

Track must be straight for the first 4" from the end of the module

Electrical sockets this end

24" — 17"

Track setback is 2½"

40" floor to top of rail

Front

Adjust + or - 1"

Main lines, 24" minimum radius, no grade

Branch line, 18" minimum radius, 1½ percent maximum grade

4"

2'-0", 4'-0", 6'-0", or 8'-0"

Parallel tracks on 1½" centers

Skyboard

14" nominal, 8" minimum

4"

Track must be straight for the first 4" from the end of the module

110V AC with ground

DC supply

Electrical plugs this end

BASIC NTRAK STANDARDS

Illustration by Rick Johnson

Alf Bossaers

This FREMO meet in Europe fills a room with many modules that are linked into a long point-to-point main line. The system's station names are mounted on the posts to help operators.

Give operation a try

Running trains with a purpose is fun, even on the smallest layouts

**BY
ANDY
SPERANDEO**

**DRAGO &
EAST RIDGE RY.**

HO scale

0 Elevation in inches

Model railroading is fun, and for many of us operation is the most fun model railroading has to offer. "Operation" can mean different things, but you'll be in the ballpark if you think of running a model railroad as if it actually made its living carrying freight and passengers.

Some people think operation is only possible on big, complex layouts, but in fact you can have a good time operating even the smallest model railroad. As an example let's look at the Drago & East Ridge Ry., a track plan by Don Reschenberg from the January 1961 MODEL RAILROADER. It's a small HO scale railroad with 18"-minimum-radius curves and no. 4 turnouts. Maybe it's not the most basic layout you could imagine, but it's still pretty simple.

The D&ER gets its odd shape from the rearrangement of a 4 x 8-foot sheet of plywood as shown in the small drawing. One advantage of this is space for a small yard across the lower end of the layout – usually on a 4 x 8 HO scale railroad the yard has to be along one side.

Imagination helps

It might look like there are only a couple of things we can do with the D&ER, namely running a train around the oval and switching the yard and industrial sidings. That's true as far as it goes, but with a bit of imagination we can arrange those simple actions into purposeful operation.

To start with, this little railroad desperately needs connections with the outside world. Let's simulate them with some train running.

The day begins on the D&ER when we back a small road engine out of the enginehouse and use it to make up an eastbound through freight in the yard. Perhaps there's a card-order system of some sort to indicate which cars are the eastbounds, or maybe we left ourselves a simple handwritten switch list at the end of our last operating session.

When the train is ready we make our air brake test and pull out, running eastward (counterclockwise) on the twice-around oval.

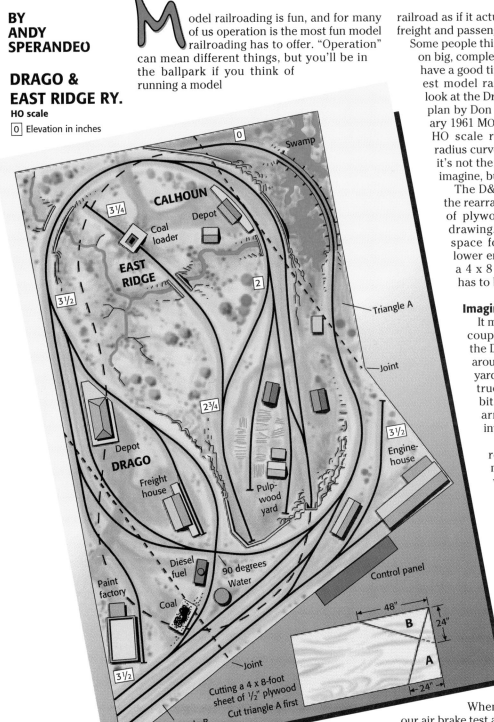